Making Room
for Mr. Right

Also by Robin and Michael Mastro

The Way of Vastu
Altars of Power and Grace

Making Room for Mr. Right

HOW TO ATTRACT THE LOVE OF YOUR LIFE

Robin and
Michael Mastro

ATRIA PAPERBACK

NEW YORK ❋ LONDON ❋ TORONTO ❋ SYDNEY

ATRIA PAPERBACK
A Division of Simon & Schuster, Inc.
1230 Avenue of the Americas
New York, NY 10020

First Atria Paperback edition January 2009

ATRIA PAPERBACK and colophon are trademarks of Simon & Schuster, Inc.

For information about special discounts for bulk purchases,
please contact Simon & Schuster Special Sales at
1-800-456-6798 or business@simonandschuster.com.

Designed by Jaime Putorti

Manufactured in the United States of America

10   9   8   7   6   5   4   3   2   1

Library of Congress Cataloging-in-Publication Data

Mastro, Robin.
   Making room for Mr. Right : how to attract the love of your life / Robin &
Michael Mastro.
      p. cm.
   1. Vastu. 2. Mate selection. 3. Women—Psychology. I. Mastro, Michael, date.
II. Title.

   BF1779.V38M394 2009
   133.3'33—dc22   2008018471

   ISBN-13: 978-1-4165-8337-0

To Kim,

May you know the sweetness of loving

your Mr. Right.

To women (and men) everywhere.

Dream the dream.

Breathe life into your vision.

Tend it with kindness and faith.

Trust in grace.

Know the universe is a benevolent

and loving place.

The moment one definitely commits oneself,

then Providence moves, too.

All sorts of things occur to help one

that would never otherwise have occurred.

A whole stream of events issue from the decision,

raising in one's favor all manner

of unforeseen incidents

and meetings and material assistance.

—W. H. MURRAY

Contents

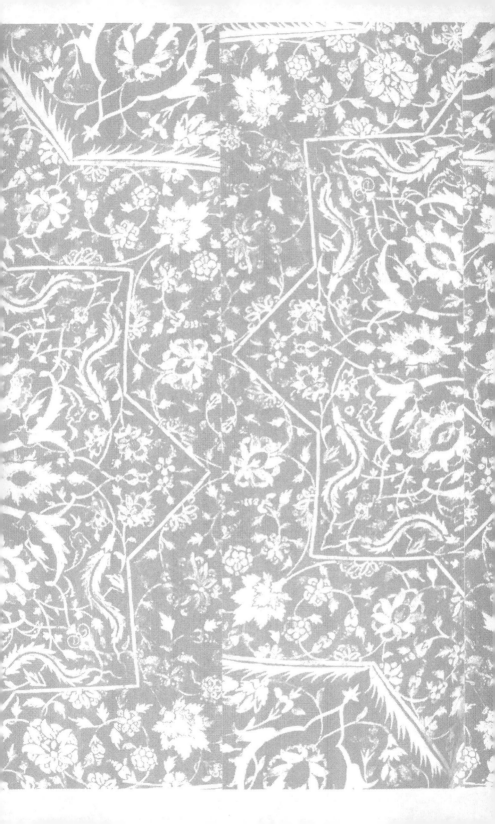

A Note from Robin and Michael

We believe in the power of love.

We experienced it early in our relationship and continue to experience it today. This book is a product of much love, and while Robin's voice will be the predominant one throughout, underneath every technique and principle is Michael's added understanding of Vastu, the science of balance and well-being. We know that Vastu can bring you the relationship you desire with just a little discipline and effort on your part. If you have been searching for love, we hope you will spend time here with us and let us help you make room for Mr. Right.

Robin

I believe that there are men in the world who understand how to love a woman in a way that makes her eyes shine and her heart sing—and I believe a woman can take charge of her life and use her power to attract that type of man. My husband, Michael, is such a man. We've been together for more than twenty years, partners in life, love, work, and now this book.

Despite my romanticism, I know my faith in love alone was not the force that brought Mr. Right into my life. I had twice married, twice divorced. The last marriage left me a single mom with a toddler to raise on my own. I felt so alone and drifted into depression.

I owned a speaker's bureau at the time. Regardless of how disconnected I felt from myself and work, the rent on my home and office came due every month. I did carry spiritual truths and metaphysical principles in my heart, but my mind flailed desperately in an attempt to figure things out. The demands of my external world made the longing for what my heart desired seem impractical and out of reach. I didn't know how to surrender to finding another way. I just kept doing what I knew how to do, which was to hold on.

Once the pressure became too great with stress coming

from too many directions—bills mounting, diapers need-
ing changing, clients calling for help, lawyers demanding I
pay attention to my divorce—I broke down. One morning
I cried out in prayer, *"Here, you take this. I feel so bad having
to say this, but I can't do this anymore. I give up. Whatever is
really mine to do, please return it. The rest is yours."* Tears
flowed, and my mind relaxed just enough to allow the
divine—call it God, Universal Good, Jesus, Muhammad,
there are many names—to take hold in my life. Then a
shift occurred within me, a connection was made, and once
again I was in touch with a source of solace and hope.

When I asked for help, I saw that, in the form of grace
and forgiveness, help had been there for me all along. I
wasn't alone, and that awareness helped me find my way
once again. I was humbled and free.

After my second marriage ended, I recovered and
healed with the help of the divine and a community of
women friends who were there for me as I was there for
them. With their help, I began to develop clarity about
what I really wanted. Some of us who were single formed
a group and engaged in a process to align our actions with
key universal principles. My transformation was steady. It
felt so good. The changes in my inner world positioned me
to receive what I desired from others, especially in a relationship with a man.

Michael

Robin and I had known each other for a few years before we became a couple. We met at a mutual friend's birthday party. We were both married to other people at the time. I was and am a developer and studied Vastu, the science of building that this book is based on, many years before, as a graduate architect. I designed spiritual centers around the world and used Vastu in designing Microsoft's first building and many buildings for the Boeing Corporation.

Robin

My first impression of Michael was his kindheartedness and his gentle ways. As we moved in the same social circles, we became friends. After our marriages ended, and unbeknownst to us, we both were becoming clear about our ideal mate by doing similar processes. I remember how surprised we were when, on our first date, we realized that we wanted the same things—to love and be loved; to raise healthy, happy children; and to do good work in the world. It wasn't long after that we fell in love and took the first steps into a lasting union.

Michael brought stability and loving acceptance into my life, which had been missing for a long time. He introduced me to a new form of spirituality, and together we became teachers of Vedic knowledge. He also introduced me to Vastu, which we initially used to help our friends and students. I went back to school, received my master's degree, and focused on making Vastu accessible in the West. Our business has flourished, and people all over the world have realized the effectiveness of Vastu in bringing love, prosperity, and happiness into their lives.

I believe that there are many Mr. Rights for each of us. Once we draw them to us, we can choose the man we want to call "the one." But I also believe that you must make the commitment to find yourself before you find him. That's really what this book is about. Once you know yourself, you can enjoy your relationships with all of the people in your life, especially Mr. Right.

Michael

Vastu is an amazing tool for accomplishing your goal. It is not a religion or a path, but a method that includes the use of natural energy to achieve well-being. It shows you how to align your actions with the positive natural forces of the universe, and consequently enhance your love life and create more of what you want.

One of the more compelling aspects of this work is that you don't have to go it alone. We'll introduce ways for you to experience the power of Vastu within your group of friends and your community as well as on your own. In fact, we encourage this, because most of us need—even long for—a group of friends, a loving community of like-minded people, in addition to a relationship with a special someone.

Robin

We've written this book in a specific order and suggest that you do the exercises in order. It's not mandatory. However, please make the first step—clearing clutter—your priority before you move on to any others.

To give you an idea of the impact of this work in the lives of women, we've invited three friends along for our journey: Sasha, Lori, and Faith. They are a blend of many of the wonderful women we've worked with over the years. Their composite stories illustrate the lives and relationship patterns we've seen in our work and show the responses we've observed, which can only be described as human.

One added note: couples can benefit from these techniques, too. The action steps are universal and work to support and improve the quality of anyone's life, married or single.

As we said at the start, we believe in the power of love. We also believe that the universe is a loving and benevolent place that extends to each of us a birthright of love. We invite you to discover this for yourself. It's time to shake out the old energy in your life and in your environment. Make room for the new. Make room for Mr. Right.

CHAPTER ONE

What Does the Environment Have to Do with It?

What if we told you that your relationships with men are impacted by the floor plan of your home? Chances are, if you are like most people we've worked with, your first reaction would be skepticism, at least until you became more familiar with Vastu Shastra, the science of harmonious living.

If you knew more about Vastu, you would realize that the floor plan of your home, among other things, influences your life and the level of satisfaction, health, productivity, and happiness you experience. According to Vastu, your floor plan also contributes to the harmony, or stress, in your life and your relationships.

If you knew even more about Vastu, you'd know that it is one of the texts found in the Vedas, an ancient body of knowledge from India, and that it was created seven thousand to ten thousand years ago by enlightened masters who observed and documented the workings of the universe. Because these workings, or natural laws, are universal, they still work today. When you learn to apply them in your home or office—wherever you spend considerable amounts of time—your life, which includes everything we've mentioned above and more, flourishes.

Let's look at a few of Vastu's key, life-changing tenets, which, for the scope of this book, we've tailored specifically to your quest for Mr. Right.

The first principle has to do with universal energy. This energy—whether you call it *qi, chi, Shakti, Rhor,* or *grace*— flows through everything that exists, everywhere. Your ability to consciously align yourself with it and be supported by it gives you great power to attract the mate, and anything else, that you desire.

Vastu Principle One

When energy flows unrestricted within your environment, that energy supports you to receive more of what you want in life—including the man of your dreams.

Everything within the universe—all that you are, all that you see, and all that is not seen—is made of energy, and that energy is contained in the five elements of earth, water, fire, air, and space. These elements are the basic building blocks of all life and matter.

Your mind, your body, the food you eat, this book, your living and working environments, all are made of these elements, which form the foundation of the underlying energy that connects us to each other. It is because of this connecting energy that we breathe the same air, drink from the same water, walk on the same earth, and enjoy the same warmth and light of the same sun. Because of this profound connection, everything influences everything else.

The elements are constantly balancing each other. The energy within each element seeks to flow without interruption and in harmony with the other elements. Therefore, an environment that is constructed or balanced to allow energy to flow unimpeded is optimal: within it you are aligned with the natural order of the universe. In such a place you feel this alignment as harmony and peacefulness; such a place holds the serenity of a sanctuary or an oasis. The essence of this feeling is a personal connection to the mysterious, sacred source of life itself. It may be a subtle feeling, but it is undeniable—you are connected to the source, and you are one with life. You experience ease and a sense of grace; what you want often comes to you with little effort.

The second principle of Vastu works with balance.

Vastu Principle Two

Eliminating stress by balancing the five elements in your environment enhances your ability to create a healthy relationship.

In nature, the five elements of earth, fire, air, water, and space are naturally in balance. But from a Vastu perspective, once a structure is built in any natural environment, the elements are disrupted, and energy becomes blocked or stuck. This causes an imbalance, or stress, which can be felt. This stress creates dis-ease in the body, mind, and spirit, which in turn manifests as negative thoughts and feelings. Stress and negative thinking block the ability to create the life you want and also can make you unhappy or even sick. Creating the life you do want is what *Making Room for Mr. Right* is all about.

So balancing the elements in your home and workplace is essential in reducing environmental stress, and necessary if you are to be totally aligned with the energy of the universe. This alignment of body, mind, and spirit supports you in creating total health and assists you in attracting and sustaining success in all areas, including your relationships.

The third principle of Vastu has to do with how our attitudes and beliefs create the world we live in.

Vastu Principle Three

Your thoughts, actions, and beliefs greatly impact your world and your ability to attract Mr. Right.

As we said in Principle Two, everything within the universe is interconnected. Thoughts are a part of "everything," and they are powerful determinants in creating what you want: what you think, you become. Your thoughts and beliefs are energy that impact the universe and influence the environment, including other people. Like magnets, or like the moon drawing the tide, your thoughts pull your future toward you. Every thought, whether positive or negative, forms the substance of the world in which you live.

When you think about a fulfilling, positive relationship,

or fulfillment on any level, your thoughts communicate to the universe that you are ready to take action to draw what you desire to you. It is so important to consciously recognize that your thoughts—as well as your beliefs and actions—now, in this moment, are creating your future. They matter. So choose, right now, to keep bringing your thoughts back, again and again, to what you want. By consciously focusing on just the thoughts and beliefs that affirm a great relationship, good health, success, prosperity, and happiness, you move away from unsatisfactory situations and experiences and open yourself to attracting a wonderful man, and so much more.

Using just these three Vastu principles and the action steps presented in this book, you have the power to connect with and channel the forces of the universe to bring you, among other things, a loving, balanced relationship.

We'll track the lives of our three composite women—Faith, Sasha, and Lori—to understand more completely how Vastu works.

CHAPTER TWO

A Community of Three

*L*ori, Faith, and Sasha are forty, fifty-five, and thirty-two, respectively. They are good friends who meet regularly to dish about their families, work, men, politics, and life. They do yoga, walk, shop, and eat together, and they find in their group relationship the kind of nurturing and love that women find so necessary.

Faith

It wasn't until she entered midlife that Faith realized her marriage of twenty-five years was over. She never thought it would turn out that way—that she would be living alone in a big house without a husband, with her children far away. But staying married to a man who was emotionally and physically absent had no appeal to her. She refused to live a lie. So when their third and last child moved out, Faith filed for divorce. She had a good lawyer and received a generous settlement. She couldn't just sit around, so she refreshed her writing talent with a copywriting course at a local college and started freelancing. She leveraged her talent and business ability into a healthy and profitable venture.

Most everything worked well in Faith's life. She adjusted to being single and stayed close to her grown children via phone and e-mail. Since the kids were scattered far and wide and hadn't started families yet, she didn't see them often. She enjoyed her freedom and eclectic array of women friends—some married, and some whose lives looked a lot like her own; most were members of the ever-expanding singles group she was a part of at her local church. She was healthy and saw herself as basically happy.

However, she wanted to be in a committed relationship with a man. That was the one area of her life that no matter how hard she tried, she never seemed to get right. Her attempts at dating were washouts. She felt like a failure, doomed to live the rest of her life alone. Over coffee after a long walk and some shopping with Lori and Sasha, she complained to them about her biggest blind spot. "I can never tell if a man is sincere," she said, feeling disappointed in herself for not being smarter about men, about relationships. They were sitting outside on a warm fall day in Kirkland, a Seattle suburb that attracts artists from all over the Northwest.

"I think it takes time to know if someone is serious," Sasha offered. "I mean, doesn't it take time to know if you're serious or not, or if they are? I'm just guessing, since I don't have much experience in this department. Don't worry, Faith, you'll find someone, I have no doubt."

"I agree," said Lori. "Maybe you need to go more slowly—get to know them more before you show how vulnerable you are."

Faith looked at her with a knowing smile. "Yeah," she said. "Even I think it's weird that I fall for every man I date. Ha! Is it *that* easy to fall in love?"

"I don't know," answered Lori. "But the disappointment doesn't seem to be worth it. There must be a better way."

"I'm impressed that you've done online dating," Sasha said, "and that you keep trying. I haven't had the nerve." She watched a couple, carrying a painting wrapped in butcher paper, sit down at the opposite table. She noticed that the couple seemed comfortable together but that they hardly looked at one another. She wondered if they were happy with each other.

"The downside of online dating," said Faith, "is that the last four men I've met online ended up being exactly alike—out for themselves and a good time, period." She stopped, considering what to say next. "Actually, I think online dating services are a wonderful way to meet people. I know several women who met their mates using them; I just don't seem to have the hang of it."

The three sat thinking about men, drinking coffee, checking out the crowd. Faith felt a familiar guilt. She didn't mention how each time a relationship cooled and the man didn't call, she pursued him, which left her feeling empty. She was critical of herself about this and couldn't share her feelings with her friends, although she wanted to. Her way of dealing with shame and embarrassment was to retreat into work and try to forget how she felt. She mused that she would give her own kids better advice than she gave herself. Faith realized that doing what she'd been doing since her divorce wasn't getting her what she wanted at all: someone to grow old with, who would love and accept her as is, and who would see her loving nature as a blessing from God.

Lori

When Lori married right out of high school, she thought it was for life. It was all so romantic, marrying her high school sweetheart, the captain of the football team who had graduated the year before her. She was popular, a positive person known for her boundless energy and openness to new things and ideas. She was always the first to embrace a new style of music or clothes. She found yoga before any of her friends and became a hatha yoga instructor. She was a born seeker, on the lookout for something that she knew, eventually, she would find.

Warm and kind, she never lacked friends and decided to share her best qualities with the world through becoming a nurse. In the early years of her marriage she went to night school to get her degree, while she worked part-time teaching yoga and also at a veterinary clinic. She and her husband struggled financially in their early years together and, soon after that time, had two girls.

When her daughters were little, Lori began reading avidly about decorating and gardening and found she had a knack for both. She loved their small home, which included two cats and a dog, that in her eyes were as much a part of the family as she, her husband, and the kids. She spent most of her spare time fixing up the house, especially the girls' rooms. She thought her life was perfect in most ways.

But when her husband began climbing the corporate ladder, he changed. He stayed out late and came home tired and, usually, drunk. She learned to adapt to the long nights alone and to raising the girls without his help. More and more it seemed to her that her husband wanted her to take on the role of his perfect corporate wife: to share the social responsibilities that his work life required, to make an impression, to support him and his success. He gradually transformed from a loving partner to a demanding boss.

After almost twenty years of living to serve her husband's needs, Lori finally freed herself and left the marriage. As the ink was drying on the divorce papers, her ex turned around and married a younger woman, leaving Lori with her girls, her house, and her pride.

It surprised her that she became so depressed after the divorce. She felt more grief than she imagined was possible. She thought it was all out of proportion to her feelings for her husband. In her heart she knew that when she healed she would find someone to love her the way she believed she deserved to be loved. But, she knew, it would take time to heal. She hoped it wouldn't take too long.

Sasha

Sasha had never been married. In fact, she had a recurring nightmare of standing at the altar in a wedding gown with an unknown man, panicking, about to say, "I do." In her mind, she was the original runaway bride. She called herself a skeptic and told her friends she hadn't found a man from whom she desired anything more than friendship or casual sex. That wasn't necessarily true, but she was afraid to admit that the men she met just didn't measure up.

Still, when she was completely honest with herself, she wanted to believe that the future could be different. She just didn't know how.

Her skepticism was natural given her background. Sasha's mother had distanced herself emotionally when Sasha was a teen. Sasha rebelled. Her anger stemmed from her parents' horrible marriage, which ended formally when she was fourteen, but which had been full of turmoil from the beginning. A sensitive, somewhat introverted, and intelligent child, Sasha had suffered when she heard her parents' frequent quarrels, and when her father moved out, she grieved silently. Her mother didn't want to hear about her daughter's pain and became more and more distant.

Sasha had few friends, no one to confide in, so she used television as her escape. She immersed herself in reruns

and old movies from the '40s and '50s. The passion, perfection, and certainty of the lives of the characters in those
movies and TV shows comforted her; everything was black
and white, easy to understand. If she had a life plan at all,
it was based on movie and TV plots—she'd marry a man
who possessed better qualities than her dad, and she and
her husband would have a house and kids, and live at least
somewhat happily ever after. She longed for the perfect,
passionate lives she saw on television.

The problem was, Sasha had placed an invisible, protective wall around herself after her parents' divorce. She
had dated a little bit, but found the boys she went out
with to be mainly interested in sex, or so boring that she
couldn't wait to get home and turn on the TV. She did
well in school, especially in computer sciences, where she
discovered that she was a whiz and knew that she would
make technology her career. She also had a flair for fashion
and was known for having a unique style in school, which
set her apart from others. Since she didn't care so much
about fitting in, that suited her just fine.

Then, when she was seventeen, she fell in love, to her surprise, with a boy at school. He was a bit like her dad—funny,
with a corny sense of humor. They dated for a year and talked
of getting married, but as they completed the last few months
of high school, they began to sense their futures looming and

the inevitable divergence of their life paths. Sasha enrolled in a nearby community college because of finances, or lack of them; he went away to another college. She suffered through the breakup by watching TV and old movies and working part-time in a vintage clothing store.

In college she excelled in computer technology and began to socialize. She slept around when she felt like it, secretly wishing she would meet someone but making herself emotionally unavailable, a trick she'd learned from her mother. After being in the working world for several years and still single, she knew that she wanted a fulfilling relationship. She wanted to love and be loved. She did not want to hide from intimacy night after night, alone, watching TV with her cat Simon—a great companion, but still . . .

When Lori discovered Vastu and the possibility it held to bring her a relationship with a wonderful man, she had to share it with Faith and Sasha. She knew that they wanted the same for themselves. Lori wasn't certain that Vastu could help, but it was clear as daylight that she and her friends needed something to push them beyond where they were. If a ten-thousand-year-old science conceived by ancient yogis could help her find a man, that was just fine with her. She was willing to try anything.

When she told Sasha and Faith about Vastu, they felt a fluttering of possibility in Lori's words. While skeptical, they agreed that together they would try it. Their best hopes and prayers were that the journey they were beginning would transform them.

Almost from their first conversation about Vastu, the women found themselves talking about it with others—family and friends at work, church, yoga, and other associations. And as their involvement progressed, they recognized that in addition to wanting a partner, they each longed for a community within which they could find another kind of much-needed love, support, and happiness.

Think about it, there must be higher love

Down in the heart or hidden in the stars above

Without it, life is a wasted time

Look inside your heart, I'll look inside mine

—STEVE WINWOOD

CHAPTER THREE

Making Room:
Clearing Out the Stuff
in Your Space

Clutter happens to the best of us. Whether we live in a multimillion-dollar home or a tiny apartment, we're all, at times, victims of our own cluttering.

But what you must know about clutter—and we're here to tell you so you can eliminate it—is that it is an impediment to creating a lasting relationship. That's right: your mess is a barrier between you and your Mr. Right. The natural energy that we talked about earlier, which flows through your home and office, gets stuck wherever there is clutter. That's why getting rid of it and staying rid of it is so important. When the energy doesn't flow, your good is held back.

Before you condemn yourself for cluttering, please know that clutter is normal. For many women, collecting and holding on to things bring a sense of enjoyment and a feeling of security. For a lot of us, a lack of organization combined with limited space, a busy schedule, and a constant inflow of paperwork, magazines, toys, books, and everything else eventually leads to chaos on the floor, in the closets, on the sofa, and in the office.

To understand how piles of stuff influence natural energy flow, imagine a river with many twists and turns. Where there are tight bends in the river (imagine your messy desk, for example), the water's energy pools and stagnates, and debris piles up, blocking the flow. Over time, as more things accumulate, the blockage becomes bigger and the river either turns into a lake (you can't find your desktop) or reroutes along a different channel (the floor, chairs—you get the picture). If the blockage is cleared, however, the river flows with renewed strength (you can focus on your work and be more effective).

In your home and office, clutter builds up in different areas and creates imbalances in your life and your energy. Wherever the clutter is, the blocked energy there prevents you from dealing clearly and effectively with whatever that area represents. This in turn creates stress that you feel in body, mind, and spirit—although you might not attribute the stress you feel to that old stack of magazines on the floor, the outdated and unused clothes in the closet, the stack of old mail on your desk, and the rest of the clutter that surrounds you. But when you think about it, sometimes it feels like the clutter in your physical surroundings takes up residence inside your mind, making clear thinking and decisive, appropriate action impossible.

The good news is that once you clear the clutter, the energy of your thoughts frees up and suddenly you have clarity, you can focus on attracting what you want in your life, including a relationship with Mr. Right. Life flows with greater ease when you physically remove obstacles that create the energetic logjam to your heart's desires.

Elemental Clutter and Mr. Right

Vastu teaches that the challenges you face in attracting Mr. Right are partially determined by where in your home clutter has accumulated. For instance, if your clutter is in the southeast, your relationships with men may lack enough passion to create real intimacy. You may have men friends, but they might not evolve into something more. Here's why.

In chapter 1 we talked about how everything is made of energy and contained in the five elements: earth, water, fire, air, and space. In addition, each element relates to, or is considered at home in, a specific direction or area—northwest, northeast, southeast, southwest, or the center.

Earth element resides in the southwest.

Water element is connected to the northeast.

Fire element is related to the southeast.

Air element is associated with the northwest.

Space element is alive in the center of any home.

So if you have clutter in the southeast, which is related to fire, your relationships with men could lack passion. It's that simple.

Similarly, clutter in the attic or basement, up or down, has specific effects. From a Vastu perspective, a buildup of stuff in the basement impacts your ability to let go of past experiences; clutter in the attic or upper floors of your home limits the potential for something, or someone, new to enter your life.

Clutter and Clearing: You and the Planets, Directions, and Elements

In Vastu, each of the eight directions—northwest, north, northeast, east, southeast, south, southwest, and west—has a very strong influence on a specific aspect of your life.

Here's more about how the directions affect you.

NORTHWEST: COMMUNICATION

Communicating is essential for a successful relationship. To communicate well, your mind must be clear.

The northwest relates to the air element and the moon. Moon energy influences the stability and clarity of the mind, which affects the ability to communicate accurately. Clutter in the northwest part of your home will cause your mind to be unsettled: you will feel off center, and your thoughts, actions, and experiences will reflect that. You will tend to say to your friends that you want to be in a relationship, but you're indecisive about what you want in a man. If this is you, check the northwest area of your home for clutter. If it's there, get rid of it. When the clutter is gone, you will be clearer about what you want and communicate more clearly. This will enhance your friend-ships and draw a healthy relationship to you.

 **MICHAEL'S VASTU TIP:** Hanging a heart-shaped chime in the northwest will move stuck energy in this direction.

NORTH: INTIMACY

Intimacy in relationships is supported by the abundant energy flowing from the north.

The north is associated with the air and water elements. The planet Mercury influences the energy of the north by creating depth and fullness in your connections with others. If this area is blocked by clutter, the potential for growth and deepening of your relationships (and finances, too) is limited. Freeing up this area will open you to rela-tionships with men (and money) that can grow in richness and intensity.

MICHAEL'S VASTU TIP: Keeping your valuables in the north helps attract more of the same.

NORTHEAST: PERSONAL GROWTH

Personal growth and attracting the man of your dreams depend on your connection to the source where spirit resides, which is associated with the northeast.

The northeast connects you to the element of water and the planet Jupiter. Jupiter influences growth and expansion, both within the self and in the depth of your relationship with the divine. Two powerful forces of nature converge in the northeast: magnetic energy from the north and ultraviolet energy from the east. These two forces merge in the northeast in a confluence of the highest vibration of energy that enters your home. Consider this energy to be a blessing from the universe. This area is a good place to sit for meditation.

When clutter accumulates in the northeast, you cannot find your center. Your connection to spirit is disrupted. This can manifest as a feeling that the men you initially find interesting lack sincerity once you get to know them.

 **MICHAEL'S VASTU TIP:** Place a fountain in this direction to stimulate growth in your spiritual life and in your relationships.

EAST: HEALTH

The health of relationships is influenced by energy from the east.

The east relates to water and fire and the light of the sun. The sun is associated with this direction. The life-giving force that comes from ultraviolet light emanating from the east feeds your body, mind, and spirit, and affects your health and outlook on life. Without health, it is difficult to enjoy all that life has to offer. When the east area of your home is cluttered, positive solar energy that is essential for good health cannot flow to you. Clearing this area will improve your health and your outlook on life; it will enhance the possibility of a healthy, balanced relationship.

 **MICHAEL'S VASTU TIP:** Facing east while working stimulates your creativity.

SOUTHEAST: PASSION

Passion, attraction, and satisfaction in relationships are influenced by the southeast.

The southeast is associated with the fire element and the planet Venus, which brings passion and enthusiasm into your life. Relationships feed on this energy—from the fire needed to sustain sexuality and intimacy to the enthusiasm that keeps a relationship interesting. Without a healthy flow of southeastern energy, your relationships will be, on some level, unsatisfying and unfulfilling. If clutter blocks the southeast, you may have difficulty sustaining passion in relationships. Freeing up the energy in this direction will give you the fire to generate interest and maintain attraction.

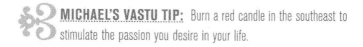 **MICHAEL'S VASTU TIP:** Burn a red candle in the southeast to stimulate the passion you desire in your life.

SOUTH: VISION AND DISCRIMINATION

Your ability to see opportunity and make good judgments about men is impacted by energy that comes from the south.

The south is associated with fire and earth. The planet Mars, with its illuminating quality, assists you in recognizing relationship and other opportunities that come your way. Flowing freely, this energy is discriminating, and boosts your ability to evaluate a relationship. When there is clutter in the south, you cannot see opportunities and act on them. Without the ability to see opportunity, to discriminate, and to make good choices, you won't realize when Mr. Right walks into your life.

MICHAEL'S VASTU TIP: Sleeping with your head to the south supports your health and ensures a better night's rest.

SOUTHWEST: STABILITY AND SECURITY

Stability and security in relationships are influenced by energy from the southwest.

The southwest relates to the earth element and Rahu, a node of the moon. Rahu's energy gives you the support you need from nature to attract and maintain a successful relationship. Without Rahu's support, you experience instability and insecurity. If you've been in a repetitive pattern of feeling unsure of yourself and doubting your ability to be in a relationship, check for clutter in the southwest. A secure, stable relationship is challenged if this area is cluttered.

MICHAEL'S VASTU TIP: To stabilize and ground your energy, place heavier furniture in the southwest area of a room.

WEST: CREATIVITY

Self-expression, self-confidence, and authenticity are associated with energy from the west.

The west is associated with the earth and air elements and the planet Saturn, which supports creative and lively relationships. Saturn energy helps you relax and enjoy the moment, encouraging you to express yourself creatively, to feel inspired, and to appreciate your uniqueness. When the west is cluttered you may lack self-confidence; you may not be able to articulate your needs, to be yourself, to let go and shine. Being comfortable within yourself is essential in attracting Mr. Right.

MICHAEL'S VASTU TIP: To stimulate your creativity, place a small crystal pyramid on the right-hand side of your desk to enhance right-brain activity.

CENTER: SUCCESS

Success in creating a relationship comes from the energy in the center of the home.

The center of your home is dominated by the space element, which influences all directions. In Vastu, the center area is considered the navel, the place from where live-giving support feeds the entire environment. Cosmic energy flows into your home to bless it through the center. If that area is cluttered, your efforts to create a relationship will not be successful. But once this area is free of clutter, all the directions benefit and you will experience more ease in attracting Mr. Right.

MICHAEL'S VASTU TIP: If there is any obstruction in the center of your home (walls, toilets, stove, fireplace, furnace), hang a twenty-millimeter clear crystal on a red string in increments of nine inches near the center to move stagnated energy.

Action Step 1
Clearing Clutter to Attract Mr. Right

Ready to get started?

We suggest you begin by clearing the area in your home that's most cluttered. We know, it's daunting. But all you need to get started is to dedicate five or ten minutes—setting an alarm clock really helps—to begin. Or, if you feel so inclined, start with thirty minutes. What is most important is that you begin!

❋ Begin with a drawer or a pile of books on the floor; or maybe a stack of magazines you've been waiting to go through; or a cabinet overflowing with old cosmetics.

❋ With each item that you pick up, ask yourself three questions: "Do I love this?" "Do I need this?" "Will I use it in the next six months to a year?"

❋ If the answer is no to any of the questions, put the item in one of three piles: the first pile is to give away; the second pile is to throw away; the third pile is to sell.

❋ When the alarm goes off, ask yourself if you are comfortable and ready to do another increment of the same amount of time.

❋ Become aware of how you feel while you are clearing the clutter. There's a great deal of energy, in the form of memories and emotions, that gets stuck in the "stuff" we own. Eliminating what is unused, unneeded, or unnecessary frees up all kinds of energy.

❋ Set aside a specific amount of time every day to work on this project until it is done.

Notice how the area that was cluttered takes on a different feeling when it is cleared. Again, pay attention to how you feel. You have freed up energy that can now be used to attract what you want, including the man of your dreams.

HELPFUL HINTS AND OBSERVATIONS
FOR THOSE WHO FEEL OVERWHELMED

If you have a great deal of clutter, you've probably been avoiding clearing it for quite some time. You might not have known its influence until now, and after reading this chapter, you want to take action. Learning about and practicing Vastu is like starting anything new—you need to commit to *yourself* to begin. Know you are bringing energy to inertia—that can take a lot of effort at first. But eventually it will become easier.

Ask for a little help from your friends. It helps to have someone watch you do the clearing, especially when you feel it's just too much. Some people ask a friend to work with them, and others hire someone with an expertise in organizing to help with clutter-clearing.

Start anywhere—just start! Once you begin, it does get easier—you may even enjoy it! It feels good because new energy is flowing into your home to benefit you. Every area that you clear will be one less area where stress is trapped.

Celebrate your efforts! Congratulate and appreciate yourself for committing to bringing new energy into your life and creating space for a wonderful relationship.

The Friends Clear Clutter

Initially you may react to using Vastu to bring Mr. Right into your life as Faith did: turned off by the idea of clearing clutter and paying attention to which direction it's in. It may seem odd or wacky, but be open. This really is the only way to gain the most from this book: try something new and see what happens.

LORI

When Lori first told Faith and Sasha about Vastu, Lori addressed Faith's concerns by explaining that Vastu allows us to experience nature in a deeper way; it demonstrates how nature influences our lives. "It's the parent of Feng Shui," she told Faith. "Monks took it to China from India. In

China they realized the truth of Vastu principles and adapted it to their culture."

"That makes sense," Faith conceded. When she and Sasha visited Lori's home after Lori de-cluttered it à la Vastu, Faith had to admit that the change in how the place felt was remarkable. And Lori sparkled—she looked radiant.

Inspired by Faith's and Sasha's reactions, Lori volunteered to help them with their clutter dilemmas. By clearing out the old, unneeded, unused, unnecessary things in their homes, they could use the formerly stuck energy for something proactive, such as attracting Mr. Right.

FAITH

Faith didn't notice her clutter, which was part of the problem: she never really saw how bad it was. When she got involved and focused on a writing project, she found the floor to be a convenient place to drop old drafts, books, pens, whatever. She secretly believed that the floor was the most practical bookshelf of all. Her bedroom was overflowing with books, and she usually had to step over them to move about the room.

She also liked to leave unopened mail on the breakfast bar, along with magazines, newspapers, sticky notes, and several pairs of sunglasses. She used her sofa as a magazine rack. You get the picture. Faith's clutter represented a lifetime of general disarray. When she told Lori that she equated clutter with creativity, Lori said, "That is so twentieth century . . ."

The three women committed a full weekend to clearing Faith's house, room by room. They started with her bedroom, the worst. It is in the south, but, while a pretty good place for a master bedroom, its positive potential was blocked because of the abundance of clutter. Clutter in the south revealed one of the problems that Faith had in relationships with men: her inability to discriminate whether the relationship had value. With this blockage it would be difficult to discern whether a man was sincerely interested.

Further cleaning revealed a mess under her bed. Lori explained that according to Vastu, disarray under the bed created restlessness in sleep and blocked the subconscious mind. When they finished in the bedroom they moved on, ruthlessly, to the next room and the next and . . .

After hours of work, Faith's house had a new feeling. Bags of clothes and reusable items for Goodwill and the Salvation Army filled the sorting area in the living room. Neat piles of books were ready to be sold at a secondhand bookstore. There were even blankets and an extra mattress ready to be picked up by the local homeless shelter. The space Faith called home felt clean and spacious. The countertops in the kitchen were visible—she hadn't seen them in years. In the bathroom, the friends had tossed so many outdated cosmetics and potions that the counters actually began to look a little bare. Her work space felt fresh and clean. Lori moved Faith's desk to face east and placed a small fountain she'd found in a spare bedroom on the northeast corner of the desk to stimulate Faith's connection with spirit and to support her abundance.

At the end of the weekend, Sasha, Lori, and Faith had accomplished something magnificent. Faith's house looked light, roomy, and welcoming instead of cramped and cluttered. Using Lori's knowledge of Vastu and her flair for moving things around, the women finished up Sunday afternoon with so much energy that they went for a long walk in the beautiful, warm, autumn evening.

SASHA

On the next weekend, Lori and Faith arrived at Sasha's apartment bright and early on Saturday morning. Like Faith, Sasha loved her stuff. Sasha's passion for anything Deco made her one-bedroom apartment a minefield of small, dust-gathering collections on every available surface. Vintage clothing flowed out of the closets and drawers onto floors and chairs. She had three prized laptops plus a desktop computer. A decision had to be made. What was she going to keep? What was she going to let go of?

Sasha knew that her passion for computers, collectibles, and clothes, especially, had gotten out of hand. She realized that her love of collecting had become an addiction, and she knew she had to decide whether she was going to continue to live with literally no room to even sit down and relax, or start unloading what she didn't love, need, or even want anymore.

Having her friends there for encouragement bolstered Sasha's resolve. But there was a big difference between seeing her own clutter and helping Faith with hers. The sacrifices Sasha faced made her uncomfortable. She cried as she contemplated what she was about to do—let go. Even though she wanted her life to change and to make room for a relationship, it was really hard to say good-bye to so many things she thought had been important. At the same time, she could see how she had wasted so much money on what she realized was junk . . . lonely junk.

Much misdirected energy underlined all of Sasha's spending. The items she purchased, although nice, didn't bring her any real satisfaction. Stuff had kept her safe, insulated, and protected from hurt and commitment. These issues came to the surface to be healed as she cleared her apartment of clutter.

So she was delighted when, with every decision to get rid of something, she actually felt a surge of new energy. It took a lot of courage for her to push through her fear, but once she got into a rhythm it was easier, especially since she now had a different perspective on what she owned.

She packed most of her collected treasures to deliver to an antique store nearby. She figured that with the money she would make from the transaction she would give herself a long weekend at a nice spa and let herself be nurtured and cared for. She definitely wouldn't use the money to go out and buy more stuff.

The women completed packing up her treasures and took them to the antique store later that afternoon. The young man who waited on them complimented Sasha on many of her collectibles. When they walked out of the store, Faith nudged Sasha and told her that the man behind the counter looked interested in her and that he was cute. "Maybe it's already working," she whispered to Sasha, who dismissed the comment, although she couldn't help noticing that he was, in fact, pretty cute.

They came back to Sasha's apartment before heading out for dinner, just to see how the place felt without all the clutter. "It feels like a new space," said Lori. Sasha gave her and Faith much-deserved hugs for their help.

"You know," Sasha told them as she looked around, "my mind feels so much clearer in here now. Did you notice before that it was hard to think in here?"

Faith nodded. "Yes, as a matter of fact . . ."

There was definitely something different and, whatever it was, it felt remarkably right.

The best and most beautiful things in this

world cannot be seen or even heard, but must

be felt with the heart.

—HELEN KELLER

CHAPTER FOUR

The Process of Attraction: Opening the Internal Pathways

Science has established that our physical reality is not solid; our physical world is composed of constant molecular movement that is influenced by our thoughts and intentions. In fact science, especially in the field of quantum physics, has proved the third principle of Vastu, one that teachers of metaphysical truths have been telling us for a long time: we are the artists of our own lives; our canvas is the world we inhabit.

We think this is great news! It means that we can make positive, conscious adjustments to the vast field of all possibility that we call life and decide exactly what we wish to create.

Robin's Experience

Years ago, as a young mother with a small child, I didn't have a clear idea of what I wanted or needed in my life. I allowed my husband at the time, who was a kind but misguided soul, to decide for our small family. Not knowing how to make decisions for myself, I went along with those he made until my world began to crumble. We divorced, and I had no choice but to pay attention and take control of my own destiny.

At that time I didn't have great tools to support my heart's desires. The ones I had were based mostly on spiritual theories and my determination to avoid emotional pain. I had much to learn, but I knew in my heart of hearts that I wanted to make choices that harvested love, not harsh lessons. Just knowing that was enough to begin my journey out of abusive, unconscious relationships and move me forward on my quest for a fulfilling, happy life, which included a loving, supportive man.

It is the heart's yearning to love and be loved that gives us hope that there is more to life than we know. The little inkling, the small voice inside that says "this can't be all there is," nourishes our faith in a future that will bring us fulfillment. Over the years I learned that we must nurture the heart's ability to create and support the vision of our desires and longings. We must *see* the possibility of something different and breathe life into our vision with action. Action is needed to step away from the revolving door of hope with no vision, which leads to sadness, disappointment, and ultimately acceptance of less than our heart's desires.

If we can only believe how much possibility the universe holds for us, we can create so much more for ourselves. In looking at my past, I now see how limited my perceptions and beliefs were about what I deserved, what I was worthy of, what I should have. I had to drop all of them to attract what I wanted, including Michael.

No doubt you are reading this book because you want to find the man of your dreams—and you can, you will. But first you need to look at your beliefs about yourself and relationships, and identify what you want in a deep and lasting relationship. In this process you will see how limited perceptions and beliefs hamper your experience. Then you will be taught a powerful technique to let go of them and move forward. Once you know what you want in your Mr. Right, you can ignite the source of attraction, that dynamic, unseen "place," the quantum field of all possibility where intention turns your dreams into reality.

This action step requires that you have faith; that you allow yourself to believe in the unseen. The workings of the universe are not understood by our conscious, waking mind, so we must open our hearts and our minds, and trust that the divine can and will fulfill our desires.

You might be thinking, "I've been wishing for a good relationship for a long time." Well, what I'm speaking of here is *more* than wishing. It is an alignment of mind, heart, and spirit that tunes in and focuses your desires, much like the dial and antenna on a radio tunes in a station and eliminates the static, or interference. Imagine having the ability to do this: you move the "dial," your thought, to what you truly desire, the "station"; and the "antenna," the energy of your conscious intention, directs to you what you want. You become the cocreator of a new reality, one in which your desire is aligned with your spirit. The trick here is to hold this intention as gently as you would a butterfly, knowing that to control it would destroy it.

A note from Michael: This action step has particular relevance to both Robin and me because, without knowing it, we were both making lists of what we wanted in partners at about the same time. Within a month of completing them, we had our first date. The rest is history.

We've seen the action step in this chapter help our clients create rich, fulfilling lives. To reap the benefits of the steps in this book, you need to make a commitment to yourself and your future that you will take the time to do them. Commitment is all-important—it is the transformative element that will change you and the world. We feel that if you are reading these words, you have arrived at the perfect place and time to do the work that will bring positive change into your life. Willingness and a sense of adventure are all that are needed to begin!

Action Step 2
The Process of Attraction

By emptying the mind and putting on paper all you believe and desire your Mr. Right to be, you open up to the energy that will bring what is yours to come forward.

Please read this chapter and chapter 5 thoroughly *before* beginning the Process of Attraction exercise, so you will understand how these processes work together.

Action Step 2 is to be done during the two weeks leading up to the full moon. It focuses on defining the qualities you want in a man and a relationship. You will do it in the evening, for seven consecutive nights, after you are ready for bed. It will be the last thing you do before sleep on each of the seven nights.

Begin each session with this . . . We suggest that you do a few minutes of a very simple breath relaxation exercise to help you relax into this action step, to open up your energy, allowing your spirit to be entirely present and available to you.

As you sit in bed, place your left palm over your heart and your right hand over the left. Inhale through your nose slowly and deeply, allowing the air to fill your lungs. Relax your arms, neck, and shoulders, and allow your stomach to slowly expand, if it wants to, as you inhale. Once your lungs are full, exhale slowly through your mouth. Do this inhalation/exhalation at least seven times, slowly.

Now, feeling relaxed, you are ready to begin.

FIRST NIGHT: MAKE SEVEN LISTS

On the first night, after you have prepared for bed and done your breathing exercise, take your pen and note-book—we suggest a small binder with loose, lined paper.

You will need seven lined pieces of paper, each marked at the top with one of these topics:

What I want in a man emotionally

What I want in a man spiritually

What I want in a man physically

What I want in a man sexually

What I want in a man intellectually

What I want in a man financially

What I want in a man socially and politically

In your relaxed state on this first night, write as much as you can on each of the seven topics above. You are emptying your mind of thoughts and desires. You can write on the front and back of each page if necessary, and if you need to add more paper for a specific topic, please do so. You will know when you are complete for the evening with each topic.

THE SIX NIGHTS THEREAFTER

On the next six evenings, again, after you are in bed and have done your breathing exercise, read over each list, refining, reviewing, adding, and subtracting. Keep the topics separate.

There are two additional topics in this action step that you will do each evening for these seven continuous nights.

CREATE A PERFECT DAY SCENARIO

The first topic has to do with creating a scenario to "feel" yourself into the relationship you desire. This is creating a story of your perfect day, from waking in the morning until falling asleep at night, with that one perfect man. Imagine it being a weekend with no one but you and your mate. Make this day as real as possible in your imagination and on paper. Mark this paper as follows:

A Day in My Life with My Mr. Right

What does that day look like?

What would you do?

Where would you go?

How would it feel?

If you cannot imagine the feeling of being with the man of your dreams, how will you ever know what you really want? Wishing for a man and knowing what you want are two very different things. With this part of the action step, you are refining the feeling tones of your experience, bringing more color and substance to your vision, which is essential in creating the experience you want in your everyday life. Again, as with the topics above, every night for seven nights keep refining your vision. Don't hesitate to add or delete.

WHAT YOU LEARNED FROM YOUR FATHER

The final exercise for this step, which is also to be done on each of the seven nights, works with the subtle and not so subtle beliefs, opinions, and judgments you learned about men from your father. Whether he is or was the best dad in the world, an absent father, or the worst father ever is not as relevant as the messages, observations, and perceptions you have gathered from the relationship.

You carry the feelings you have for and about your father into your life as you grow into womanhood. By the time you are an adult, your relationships with men in general and with the men you bring into your heart are greatly influenced by your father. How you think and feel about him influences how you feel about yourself and men. On this piece of paper write:

What I Have Learned About Men from My Father

Writing on this topic will help you understand parts of yourself that may have gone unnoticed or unresolved for years. It was revelatory for me when I did it more than twenty years ago. Although I was aware of feelings and ideas I had about my father and recalled emotional experiences with him, I had not realized how much my unconscious judgments about him were impacting my relationships and how they determined the kind of men I was attracting. After doing this exercise, a light went on within me and a tremendous shift occurred in my thinking and emotions. So it has been with our clients through the years, and so may it be with you.

WHILE YOU SLEEP . . .

Every night, sleep with the pages near you—put them on your nightstand or on the floor near your bed. Words have tremendous energy and work on many levels. While focusing on this exercise, your mind, body, breath, intellect, memory, emotions, and spirit are all engaged with the powerful words you have written. As you sleep, the mysterious and transforming work continues, shifting the energy of inertia into something new, vital, and desired in your physical experience.

THE EIGHTH DAY

On the morning of the eighth day, wrap your completed list in a piece of silk (either a scarf or a piece of fabric) and place it in a drawer or other safe place where it will be undisturbed. You will use the list during the Full Moon Altar Action Step, explained in chapter 5, on the evening of the next full moon.

Helpful hints and observations for those who feel uncertain and/or overwhelmed by the process.

If you feel uncomfortable initiating this task, here is a way to begin: Close your eyes, and take a few deep breaths in through your nose, and breathe out, slowly, through your mouth. Allow yourself to relax, to let go of any tension in your mind and body. When you feel settled, begin writing whatever feelings, fears, or anxieties you notice regarding this process. Just write it all out.

If for any reason you can't write, sit comfortably for five minutes with your spine erect; do some long, deep, slow breathing in through the nose, exhaling through the mouth.

Breathe with the intention of delinking your mind from stressful thoughts and letting go of tension. Say *"Ahhhhhh"* and, as you exhale, observe the energy in the areas of the pelvis, stomach, and heart. Imagine the energy moving up and out along with the sound you make as you exhale.

Let go of the fear . . . and ask for help when you need it! Fear, hesitation, and anxiety reside in the mind. Write it out or call a friend and talk it out. A support group of women friends can help you move through these processes. My women friends helped me by being present when the fear and the uncertainty came up. Asking for help from others and from your own spirit through writing will make the road much smoother if you feel resistance.

No excuses—just begin! You might find a hundred and one things to do to avoid this action step, but I assure you nothing is more important than knowing what you want and being clear that it is *your* desire, not someone else's. Just do it; let all the excuses fall away. This is for you, and you are worth it!

Celebrate your beginnings and endings and every day in between! Now is the time to admire and appreciate what you are doing for yourself. You are amazing and thoroughly lovable! Treasure your efforts; you are opening the channels of energy so that transformation can occur. A new life is on the way and change is in the air!

Let's see what Faith, Sasha, and Lori experienced with this exercise.

Asking for What the Heart Desires

FAITH

On an early fall day, sitting with her morning tea, Faith was about to surprise herself by being the first of the three to begin the Process of Attraction. She looked at the astrological calendar next to the kitchen phone on the wall to confirm that she was within the two-week period leading up to the full moon.

She mused about the fact that it was only a couple of weeks earlier that she had given Lori a hard time about Vastu, and now she was taking the lead. But she had been through so many half-baked, disappointing relationships that she was more than ready to look at what she felt she had turned into: a failure in the men department.

She feared change, but she had decided to be open to

doing the work and letting go of any thoughts and beliefs that blocked her from having happy, healthy relationships.

That evening, after getting ready for bed, Faith gathered up the special pen she had bought and her notebook, and hopped into bed. After propping herself up with extra pillows for the breathing exercises, she lit a candle on her bedside table. Gazing at the flame, she said a little prayer that the work would yield positive results. She then closed her eyes and took deep, slow breaths in through her nose and out through her mouth. When she opened her eyes again, five minutes had effortlessly passed.

You might notice, as Faith did, that you hold a lot of tension in your body in the form of stiffness or achiness. After taking a quick survey of how she felt, Faith noted that the tension was gone from her face, neck, shoulders, belly, pelvis, and legs. She was impressed at how simple yet profound just breathing slowly in through the nose and out through the mouth could be.

She then picked up her pen and notebook and began making her lists. After titling each of the pages with the subject matter, she wrote, page after page, topic by topic. She went back through the pages several times as new thoughts occurred to her.

An hour flew by quickly. She realized she had never thought about any of this before. She reminisced about all the men she had been attracted to, dated, and been disappointed with or by. She realized that she saw only their looks and personality and hadn't asked herself what she wanted that was any deeper than that. In retrospect, she mused, it had been as if she were reaching into a magic hat hoping she'd pull out the perfect white rabbit.

Before she turned off the lights to go to sleep, she put her pages next to her pillow and, as she fell asleep, she had an unusual and lovely sensation of energy in her heart. She almost imagined a little light there that had suddenly become brighter.

A few days later, Lori and Sasha began their work with the Process of Attraction. They found the exercise illuminating and, like Faith, were amazed at how little they knew about what they wanted in a man or in a relationship.

The Women Meet

When the three met for a quick lunch to check in, Faith confided in Lori and Sasha how uncomfortable it made her feel to consider her own needs, having been raised to be more concerned about how others felt. She also mentioned that through doing this exercise, she felt that she wasn't alone—she felt peace in her heart, like she was really there for herself.

SASHA

Sasha told her friends that she had had a revelation about her parents' separation. Plain and simple, she had blamed her mother for her father leaving. When she wrote down all that she had learned from her father, she revisited that lonely time in her life where she used TV to block out the pain of loneliness and isolation. For the first time she looked squarely at her father's imperfection and betrayal, and accepted her mother's anger and depression as understandable responses to her father's unfaithfulness. She saw, too, that having grown up in such an unstable home environment, she believed men were not to be trusted. Eventually they would leave.

Sasha also realized that her pattern was to act aloof and unavailable like her mother, if men did get too close. This behavior kept her safe, but lonely. She didn't want to protect herself from imagined hurt any longer.

"So after doing this step, I thought about everything that's happened so far since we've been doing Vastu," Sasha said as she looked from one friend to the other. "I thought about how great my apartment feels after decluttering, and I'm no longer skeptical—there really is something to this."

Faith nodded. Lori smiled.

"I believe," Sasha continued, "that I can change—I really think I can let a man get close now. I believe that. Who would have thought? There is hope for me! And if there's hope for me, ladies, there's hope for anybody!"

LORI

Lori reminded her friends that, like clearing clutter from their homes, they were "cleaning house" inside themselves when they did the Process of Attraction.

With the needs of her two teenage daughters, Emma and Ava, and the sheer amount of activities that filled her daily life, Lori hadn't spent much time reflecting on herself or her desires. In her process, she confronted unresolved feelings about her divorce, and realized that it was time to consider a change in how she filled her day. Maybe it was even time to start dating.

As she wrote about her day with Mr. Right, Lori had moments of doubt about her sanity. She wondered if the kind of day she was thinking of was really in the cards for her. She could not imagine how she could get there from where she was. Would there be a man who would want to be with a woman with two teenage daughters and an extended social network of friends and colleagues that were more like family? She realized that she had filled her time so as not to feel loneliness, in the same way that Sasha had filled her apartment with collectibles and Faith had filled her house with clutter.

She told Faith and Sasha how she'd doubted her sanity for a moment. "Then I remembered to breathe," she said, "and I thought, who's to say if what we're doing isn't the sanest thing we could be doing? How crazy is it to just *wish* for a great relationship and do nothing about it? I'm beginning to think this is the most proactive thing I've ever done, even if it did seem uncomfortable at times while I was doing it—to look at what I want and then prepare myself, my home, and my heart for someone wonderful, even if it does feel, in this moment, rather far-fetched."

The three friends agreed that it was crazy to wish for everything to be perfect and expect that somehow, miraculously, Mr. Right would appear. It was a much more positive and empowering statement to do something, such as Vastu.

"I so want to tell a couple of my friends in my church group about this." Faith sighed, thinking of the women who meant so much to her. "They're like me: around my age, really great, beautiful women who are so full of life, but they're alone. I know they could use this."

Lori smiled enthusiastically. "Why don't you, then? I'd

like to tell some of my other friends, too. I think we should share this with others. It could be helpful. I've thought of talking to some members of my yoga class about it."

Sasha shook her head. "I can't think of anyone to tell except Corrine at work," she said. "I'm her supervisor, but I think she would be open to it. I'm sure it would help the entire office immensely if another person was doing this. I'm going to mention it . . ."

As the women finished their lunch, each thought of future possibilities and reflected on the changes that were already beginning to take place.

> Your task is not to seek for love, but merely to
>
> seek and find all the barriers within yourself
>
> that you have built against it.
>
> —Rumi

CHAPTER FIVE

The Power of the Full Moon Altar: Igniting the Source

many of us find we have internal barriers to love that seem impossible to overcome. Vastu helps dissolve these barriers, which are often simply stuck psychic energy we've been holding on to for a long time. If we want to let go, we can.

Vastu uses altars in a very scientific way to assist in opening channels that have been closed or blocked. All cultures and many religious traditions use some kind of altar as a connecting point to the higher, unseen powers of the universe. These wonderful and iconic creations represent the universe in perfect order. At an altar, we can humbly offer our challenges as well as our hopes, dreams, and desires. Your altar is sacred ground where you can unburden your soul in times of need and ask for support and fulfillment.

Robin's Story

My introduction to altars and their influence began after I had lost nearly everything—car, home, belongings—three times. During this cycle my ex-husband, in his quest for financial success, gambled away our savings, our home, and our possessions. Toward the end I was left homeless with my infant daughter. Because I was, and am, blessed with a network of kind and loving friends, we had a place to stay until we regained our footing. I felt an all-encompassing gratitude when, once again, I had a place to call home.

At the time I knew about yoga and meditation. I loved the feeling of diving deep into the self, using the tools and techniques of yoga, but I was undisciplined, distracted, and inconsistent in my commitment to spiritual pursuits. My focus, as a young mother, was not so much on inner growth, and I didn't choose to make the commitment to the solitary pursuit of knowing myself. I didn't understand that the rewards of spiritual work are not always obvious or immediate, nor did I understand how a spiritual practice could alleviate the stress and strain of my turbulent life. And because I was focused on family and our immediate needs, I chose to search for union and fulfillment outside of myself.

It took the real humbling of losing home and belongings for me to learn what really matters in life. One of the great things about the adversity I experienced was that it caused me to reinitiate my spiritual practices with gratitude for the completion of the tough lessons I had finally learned. It was during meditation that I had a life-changing vision. In it, I had walked through a door and was standing on the edge of a forest watching a group of people dressed in unusual clothing. They were gathered under the full moon to honor nature and to ask for her support during the next moon cycle. They stood in a circle surrounding an altar they were creating on the ground. The elements of earth, air, water, fire, and space were lovingly represented by items gathered from forests and fields, mountains and rivers. In the center of the altar was a hammered chalice illuminated by the full moon. Within this central container, each participant placed his or her most precious valuables, surrendering them to be energized by the light of the moon. They began chanting words in a foreign tongue, but the meaning of what they were saying was clear to me.

The effects of this experience lasted long after it was over.

The following full moon, I made an altar that replicated the one in my vision. On it I placed representations of the elements in the pattern I had seen, surrounding a central vessel. Since I didn't own a hammered chalice made of precious metal, I took aluminum foil and molded it over my salad bowl. Within the bowl I placed items that were valuable to me: my favorite jewelry, my wallet, and my checkbook. I placed a written message on an unlined piece of paper asking the divine to love and sustain my family. Closing my eyes, I gave thanks to the universe for its continued support.

Every month, for well over twenty years, I have done this process on the full moon, either alone or with Michael, or with a whole group of friends. It has alleviated my suffering and uplifted my spirit; it has brought seeming miracles to the lives of all of us.

Years after I made my first altar, when I was a graduate student in Whole Systems Design, I traveled to Egypt and India to study their ancient cultures. My interest eventually focused on Vastu, which had deeply inspired me in my personal relationship with Michael. I knew I could bring its principles to people in a way that was accessible, easy to use, and that yielded results. Taking the most potent aspects of the science, I applied them to creating small environments, which I called altars, based on Vastu principles. I believed that they could have a transformational influence on people's lives and help uplift humanity. I wanted to help people better their lives through the principles of Vastu and make this my life's work. Over the years, various forms of these Vastu altars have provided positive change and forward motion for people with whom we have worked throughout the world.

In this chapter we'll show you how to create an altar using the power of the full moon to ignite your highest aspirations and bring them into physical form.

The Full Moon Altar

This altar attracts potent blessings from the divine. It is like a homing device for your hopes and dreams, sending its message to the universal benevolent forces that you are open, willing, and ready to receive blessings. It supports your ongoing happiness and gratitude, and revs up the attraction energy throughout the coming month.

YOUR HEART'S DESIRES: THE ALCHEMY OF MANIFESTATION

The Full Moon Altar amplifies whatever you offer it. The essential element in the process of attracting fulfilling love is gratitude, so when you offer gratitude during the ceremony presented in this chapter, you energize the manifestation of your deepest desires. When you live with a grateful heart, others are drawn to you and feel uplifted in your presence. Gratitude creates happiness; it energizes and purifies your mind, body, and spirit; it transforms your inner and outer world. Gratitude allows you to become the love you wish to receive.

Action Step 3
Creating Your Full Moon Altar

You can make the Full Moon Altar personal and just for you, or you can invite a group of friends over who also are working on creating fulfilling relationships. Building community has a synergistic affect on the Process of Attraction and yields remarkable results. Make this altar a monthly ritual and enjoy the ongoing benefits that connecting with the abundant energy of the full moon brings.

INSTRUCTIONS FOR CREATING YOUR ALTAR

Time

Assemble the Full Moon Altar early in the evening that leads up to the full moon, and remove it the following day.

For example, if the moon is full at 10:30 A.M., put the altar up the night before. If it is full at 10:30 P.M., create it earlier that evening.

Location

You may place the altar outside, where the full moon energy is most enlivening, or indoors, on a table near a window. If placed indoors, it is best, if possible, that moonlight touches the altar, even symbolically, to enliven it with magnetic lunar energy. Even on a cloudy evening, the magnetic energy of a full moon can be felt.

If the altar is inside and others participate, place it on a coffee table or dining table so the group can gather around it.

We've had large groups assemble in an open area under a central skylight between our dining and living rooms where we have created a three-tiered altar just for the occasion.

 MICHAEL'S VASTU TIP: The Full Moon Altar is a wonderful place to purify and cleanse—as moon energy is very purifying—anything important to you. One suggestion is to place jewelry you wear daily—rings, necklaces, bracelets, etc.—on the altar.

WHAT'S NEEDED

Each of the five elements of earth, air, water, fire, and space must be represented and placed in the proper direction on the altar. You will need a compass to position the elements. Since this altar is erected and taken down within a day, the altar itself is not directionally placed. We will talk more about the use of direction in chapter 6, when you create your Relationship Altar.

❁ The *earth* element is placed in the southwest. Use crystals, seeds, rocks, a plant, a bowl of rice, or anything that comes from the earth to represent the earth element.

❁ The *air* element is located in the northwest. Consider incense, a feather or feathers, standing wind chimes, a fan, or a bell as symbolic of this element.

❁ The *water* element is in the northeast. A clear, translucent, or lightly colored vase (in blue or yellow) with water and fresh flowers, a bowl or cup of water, or a fountain can be used.

❁ The *fire* element is in the southeast. A candle or incense can be used as items to represent this element.

❋ The *space* element is in the center of the altar. Use a small plate or a bowl made of metal or glass. We call this the *offering tray*. The surface should be reflective so that, even symbolically, it will reflect the light of the moon. Here you will place your request to the divine for your Mr. Right. More about this on page 71.

THE ELEMENT OF BEAUTY

Beauty is not, per se, an element like air, earth, water, fire, or space, but it is an essential principle of Vastu and fundamental to the enjoyment of life. It is a quality of the divine associated with wealth of all kinds—physical, material, emotional, and spiritual. Beauty is achieved through balancing the five elements; its influence radiates in the enlivened, purified atmosphere and is experienced as peace, harmony, and pleasure.

In this step you will create a beautiful altar and add to it your appreciation, which will awaken its supportive energy. Appreciation and gratitude are alchemical keys that unlock the unlimited potential of the universe and give you direct access to the divine forces that can assist you in transforming your life. Your altar links you to the benevolent universal energies that are helping you attract your Mr. Right.

Layout for the Full Moon Altar

~ North~

NW			NE
a	p	w	
	o		
e		f	
SW			SE

a = Air

p = Personal Symbol

w = Water

o = Space

e = Earth

f = Fire

POINTS OF REFINEMENT

❀ Before setting up your altar, make sure the area that it will be placed on is clean.

❀ Use the colors of light blue and yellow for either the pieces that represent the elements or the accent pieces. These colors are indicative of moon energy. You also can add the metal silver, the semiprecious moonstone, as well as pearls, to enhance the feeling of your altar.

❀ Once the elements of earth, air, water, fire, and space are in place, add a personal symbol on the altar. Place it in the center, right behind the offering tray. Personal symbols could be a collage of pictures cut from magazines that illustrate your desires, or a photograph that evokes feelings of happiness or fulfillment. You also can add a statue of Parvati, the sacred Mother Goddess from India; a picture of Radha and Krishna, who are Vedic aspects of the divine and represent devotional love; or any statue, icon, or item that evokes in you a feeling of love, grace, and fulfillment.

YANTRAS AND MANTRAS: TOOLS FOR ACTIVATING YOUR ALTAR

In the Vedic tradition, mantras are subtle sounds that move energy through vibratory frequencies. They are driving forces of manifestation. Yantras are geometric representations of mantras, or sound made visible, that emit frequencies. There are thousands of yantras and corresponding mantras, and each has a direct, specific, and powerful effect on the body, mind, spirit, and surrounding environment.

Here is the Moon Yantra and its corresponding Moon Mantra. Both are specific for your Full Moon Altar ceremony. You will use them to "ignite" your altar (see "Enlivening Your Altar" later in this chapter).

Moon Yantra

For a free, downloadable version of this yantra and to hear the mantra chanted, a special Web page has been created just for you. To access this page, go to *www.makingroom formrright.com/freeyantra*.

Mantra:
Om Namo Bhagavate Vasudevaya Namaha

Phonetic pronunciation:
Om Na-mo Ba-ga-va-tay Va-su-day-vai-ya Na-ma-ha

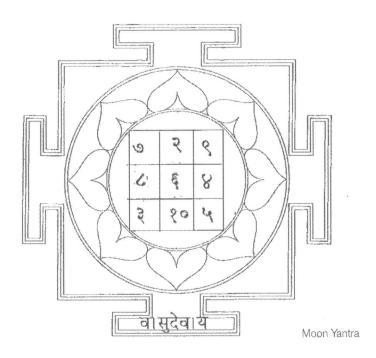

Moon Yantra

BEFORE THE CEREMONY

✽ Be sure to be freshly bathed and to wear clean clothes for this ceremony.

✽ Take the lists you created in chapter 4 and read them over once again. You will be synthesizing all of your writing into three potent words that represent the feeling tone of what you want—the end result of all that you imagine your Mr. Right to be. Write these words on a small, unlined piece of paper. You will be offering this paper to the divine by placing it in the offering tray on the Full Moon Altar as part of the activation ceremony.

✽ Download and print out the Moon Yantra from the Web site, and remove the extraneous paper by cutting out the square yantra shape. You will be using this yantra to ignite the altar. (*Note:* Only one yantra is needed for the ceremony, even if there is a group of people.) Listen to the mantra on the Web site, also. You and everyone in your gathering will be saying this mantra nine times as part of the ceremony to ignite the altar.

✽ If others will be joining you—and we encourage you to invite others to participate—ask each person to bring an item for the altar. Before the ceremony begins, participants can place their offerings on the altar. Over the years we have seen how significant it is when people add something special to them. Our friends have brought everything from personal poems to the visionary words of Native American elders. Flowers, shells, or rocks from faraway lands also have been added. One woman placed her grandmother's recipe for love on the altar.

❀ Let everyone who is participating know that whatever is spoken within the circle is to be honored and held as sacred. It is essential that all participants respect and honor each other and the ceremony.

ENLIVENING YOUR ALTAR: THE ACTIVATION CEREMONY

❀ Stand or kneel in front of your altar.

❀ Light a candle or candles and/or incense.

❀ If you have a bell or chimes on your altar, ring them now. Their sound purifies the environment and enlivens subtle energy within your body, bringing your awareness to the present moment—the place where transformation occurs.

❀ Pause to reflect on gratitude for what has brought you to your altar at this time. Inwardly offer respect to the moon and the forces of nature that bring possibility and fulfillment into your life through their energy, power, and grace.

❀ Hold your piece of paper with the three words that symbolize the feeling of being in relationship with your Mr. Right in your left hand, covered by your right hand, over your heart.

❀ Infuse the words with your desires by taking the following steps:

❀ First, take a few deep breaths in through the nose and out through the mouth.

❀ Continue to do this breathing technique as you imagine the three words you've written and all they represent to you.

❀ Feel these words with emotion, building the feeling within the region of your heart as you continue your breathing.

❀ When your heart feels filled with your desire, imagine that with each exhalation you are infusing the small piece of paper you are holding with the energy of your dreams and desires and your prayer for their fulfillment.

❀ Once the paper feels saturated with your request, say the three words out loud with feeling.

❀ Place the paper on the offering tray.

❀ If you are doing this action step with others, each person will do the process, either speaking the words aloud or silently.

IGNITING YOUR FULL MOON ALTAR

❀ Appoint one person to lead. The appointed leader will hold the Moon Yantra in her right hand and request that everyone close their eyes and take ten to twelve long, slow breaths in through the nose and out through the mouth.

❀ The leader will then ask everyone to focus on experiencing the feeling of having their heart's desires met. This is not the time to focus on specifics, but on the end feelings, or emotions, such as happiness, contentment, fulfillment, and love.

❀ Place the Moon Yantra in the offering tray, on

top of the pieces of paper
already there.

❁ Instruct everyone to do
the following: using your
right hand, extend the
small (pinkie) finger and
the index finger, folding in
the other two fingers
against your palm, placing
your thumb over the top

Mudra to Activate Full Moon Altar

of the folded fingers to hold them in place. This is a
mudra, a Sanskrit word that means a hand position
that moves energy in a specific pattern.

❁ With everyone's hand in this position, face the
altar, and move your arm from the elbow forward
and back nine times, pointing the fingers, as the arm
comes down, toward the offering tray. For each of
the nine times you extend your arm toward the altar,
say the Moon Mantra with passion and intensity:

Mantra:

Om Namo Bhagavate Vasudevaya Namaha

Phonetic pronunciation:

Om Na-mo Ba-ga-va-tay Va-su-day-vai-ya Na-ma-ha

❀ Once you have completed this process, the altar is ignited.

❀ Afterward, we suggest that you close your eyes for a few moments of silence, or sing a song, or chant some mantras.

❀ Then go around the circle and let each person share the meaning of what she brought for the altar. Some people may not want to, and that's fine.

❀ Once the ceremony is complete and before everyone leaves, remind them to take their items home with them. These precious mementos are infused with powerful energy and can be placed on any altar, especially a Relationship Altar (more on this in chapter 6).

❀ After the guests leave, take the pieces of paper and place them in a fireproof vessel or fireplace and burn them to ashes. Do this step carefully. As the paper is burning, say a little prayer for ongoing support throughout the coming month.

Trust the process—let go of the outcome. All the activities leading up to this point have been done to bring you to the door of the great unknown and to release what you have held in your heart, mind, and soul. Trust in the perfection of your surrender, allowing the divine to be in charge of your life.

Relax, enjoy, and let go of the doubt. Remember: you are not the doer, so relax! Enjoy this time of completion. Imagine the universe is filled with wonderful surprises that come to you as you relax and enjoy life in each moment. Doubts block joy and force energy downward. From now on, whenever you feel uncertain, think thoughts that uplift your spirit. Soon your feelings will follow.

Create a positive community of support. One key to maintaining positive feelings is good company. Surround yourself with positive, like-minded people who inspire and support you as you allow the universal forces to work their magic.

Faith, Lori, and Sasha are getting ready to create their Full Moon Ceremony. Let's join them and see what happens.

The Man and the Moon:
The Women's Full Moon Altar Celebration

Faith, Lori, and Sasha prepared for the ceremony by reviewing what they'd done so far: the seven lists, the Perfect Day Scenario with Mr. Right, the writings about their fathers. Each had thought of three words that encapsulated all she offered to the altar and the divine on the full moon night.

FAITH

Faith sat on her bed with the neatly organized notebook that held her writings, amazed at what she'd written and also a little doubtful that the whole endeavor would make a difference. "God! What was I thinking?" she mused as she looked over her lists, the lessons learned inadvertently from her father, and her Perfect Day Scenario. An old doubt crept up: "I can't imagine that the universe would be all that interested in what I want." She caught herself and stopped.

"Wait!" she said out loud. She took a deep breath, something she remembered to do more and more. "Look at how you're treating yourself as you're about to offer your hopes and dreams for Mr. Right to the divine." She turned her attention to breathing again and took a deep breath in and out to calm down. It worked.

She smiled to herself. Better to keep a light heart, she thought, and laughed a little about traveling down the familiar road of self-doubt. She silently thanked herself for not ruining the night before it began.

MICHAEL'S VASTU TIP: Faith's response was not unusual. You can stop yourself with doubt and fear. The discomfort of moving forward into new, uncharted territory can bring anxiety and hesitation. In moments like these, do what Faith did: relax and take a deep breath in and out. No one can control the future; let it unfold with grace and ease.

After catching herself, Faith plowed ahead with renewed energy and finished her three-word synthesis easily. She then played a CD that she called her "nice and flowy" music. As she danced through her home, she picked up objects to place on the altar for the Full Moon Ceremony.

The altar had taken shape easily. Using the Full Moon Altar layout that Lori had e-mailed her, Faith had created an altar of beauty, enhanced with some heart-shaped seashells that belonged to her mother and a delicate, lacy doily that was her grandmother's. She really admired it. I love this! she

Faith's Heart-Shaped Shells

thought. Now it feels like Mom and Grandma are here, like I'm doing this for them, too. As she put the finishing touches on the altar, she thought about her maternal lineage. The thought that the altar was for all the women in her family—past, present, and future—moved her deeply. The thought was outrageous in a way, something she would never have considered before. Maybe Vastu is opening my mind to thinking differently after all, she mused. She felt sure that her ancestors would have approved of what she was doing, would in fact have cheered her on.

SASHA

Sasha admitted to Lori and Faith that she had been un-comfortable reading over her seven lists, thinking about the lessons learned from her father and the Perfect Day

Scenario. She resisted it intensely, as it brought up uncomfortable emotions. She felt the same doubt that Faith had, and also a vulnerability that made her tense.

Faith commiserated with her, admitting it had happened to her, too. There had been some relief in knowing that they were all working through similar fears. "Sometimes I wonder where I learned to be so critical, but I'm pleased to say that when I stopped beating up on myself for questioning the right I had to even ask for what I wanted, the doubt vanished." Faith rubbed her forehead and then smiled. "I'd say we're doing pretty well if we're able to talk about these things with each other and be honest about how we're feeling as we're doing this."

MICHAEL'S VASTU TIP: Place a small statue of Ganesh, known as the remover of obstacles in Vedic cultures, on your nightstand to remind you that you are overcoming hesitation and fear of the future.

LORI

Lori felt it was natural to doubt; it certainly was familiar. When you've doubted everything—yourself, your right to have the life you've wanted, your belief in something greater than yourself, your future happiness, just about anything and everything—for a long, long time, it becomes second nature. At least, she thought, she now recognized doubt when it arose, so she could identify it and set it aside. She knew that the three of them had come a long way. "Our hearts are open, we're in good places and in good company. We're taking responsibility and cleaning up our acts," she said to Sasha and Faith before the Full Moon Ceremony.

THE CONSCIOUS GIFT

The friends gathered at Faith's and admired the altar she'd made. Faith explained to them that she had gone through her house looking for meaningful things to place on the altar. After the five elements, the offering tray, and the personal symbol—a collage of pictures of great-looking men she pulled out of magazines—she pointed out the seashells of her mother's, and her grandmother's doily. "They made me think that I am doing this for them as well as for myself," she said to Sasha and Lori.

The concept struck Sasha as interesting. "I guess if you imagine that existence isn't limited only to this dimension—that's what scientists are saying—then what we do can benefit and influence generations before and after us.

It's like saying that, by healing our own wounds, we heal the wounds of our parents and their parents before them. What we do now can impact our children and their children, and so on."

"Well, yes," Faith agreed, "and we can pass things on unconsciously, if we just keep doing what we've always done, without thinking about how it affects us or others. I want to consciously choose my actions now and break the old, predictable cycles of self-doubt, unhappiness, and frustration."

"I've thought about this a lot," said Lori. "If we go through life like robots, just doing things because we've always done them, feeling things because we've always felt them, what can we expect but what we've always known? We simply replicate what has come before us unless we ask ourselves what we want or need." She looked at her friends. "This is *so* great—because I know that whatever we're doing is going to change us for the better, and that's what we will pass on to all the generations before and after us."

THE CEREMONY

The women gathered around Faith's altar, which she'd placed on the coffee table in her living room. Lori added the wedding ring from her marriage to the altar, and Sasha placed her personal symbol next to a statue of Ganesh.

Sasha had downloaded and printed the Moon Yantra for the ceremony, and Lori, who led it, placed the yantra on the corner of the coffee table near her. Lori chanted the mantra to ignite the yantra a few times through so they were familiar with it before she began the ceremony. It's good to do this with people who aren't familiar with the pronunciation.

Lori reminded her friends that their circle was sacred— it held their deepest desires—and that what they shared was to be honored and held as sacred. After lighting the incense and candles, she rang the bell and waited until the last thread of sound had dissolved into the air before she placed the bell back on the table. She then closed her eyes and took her paper with her three words in her left hand and placed it over her heart, crossing it with her right hand.

MICHAEL'S VASTU TIP: The placement of the hands on your heart is specific and essential. The left hand is receptive. Holding the paper to the heart with this hand is symbolic of the feminine energy and your willingness to surrender your agendas and outcome to a power other than your conscious mind. The right hand symbolizes masculine energy and intentional action. Together they embody openness and the willingness to act when the time is right.

Lori took several deep breaths in through her nose and out her mouth, and imagined the three words she held. She focused the energy in her heart region, and gently felt the force of emotion and the meaning of the words and the desire they represented. When the energy was full in her heart, she imagined that she infused the paper with all her emotions and all her dreams for the future, and saturated it with her request. She passionately spoke the words "Love, respect, companionship," then placed the paper in the offering tray.

When it was Faith's turn, she closed her eyes and did the breathing process, infusing her paper with her dreams and desires. She spoke her three words, also with passion— "Kindness, humor, fulfillment"—and placed the piece of paper in the offering tray.

Finally, Sasha closed her eyes and began to breathe as her friends held the space for her to ask for her desires to be fulfilled. She built the energy in her heart and allowed the energy to merge with the paper. She spoke her three words—"Honesty, openness, tenderness"—and placed her paper on top of the other two already in the offering tray.

Lori picked up the Moon Yantra in her right hand and asked the others to close their eyes and take a dozen long, slow breaths in through the nose and out the mouth. She kept count. After they completed the breathing, Lori spoke in a quiet voice. "Now, imagine what it will feel like to have all your desires met. Feel this feeling, just the power of these words that are written on your papers."

Each woman smiled; some tears of happiness welled in Sasha's eyes. Then Lori instructed her friends to open their eyes, and she placed the Moon Yantra onto the offering tray, on top of the written papers. She asked Faith and Sasha to make the mudra with their right hands and they chanted the mantra *Om Namo Bhagavate Vasudevaya Namaha* in unison, passionately, nine times, as they moved their hands back and forth toward the offering tray.

Once they finished the ceremony, Faith broke into song—"Amazing Grace" arose straight from her heart, and Sasha and Lori joined in, feeling gratitude for the ceremony and for their bond of friendship and love. After the last note they sat, their bodies pulsating with the vibrant energy that filled the room.

Lori shared with Faith and Sasha that the wedding ring she placed on the altar was originally her grandmother's ring. She and her ex-husband didn't have any money to buy one, so her grandmother gave them hers. Lori loved the ring and felt the ceremony would purify it of the sadness it held from the years she wasn't happy in the marriage. She wanted it to be filled with love so she could pass it on to one of her daughters when the time was right.

Sasha had brought a piece she loved from her Deco collection, something she had saved from the day they had cleared clutter in her apartment. It was a small figurine of a woman swinging on a swing attached to a crescent moon. "It represents my desire to be attached to the power of the moon, to dream my dreams into reality," she said.

They had tea, and then Lori and Sasha hugged Faith good night and walked into the full moon night to go home and contemplate what they had just done. After she closed the door, Faith removed the Moon Yantra from the altar and put it on the fireplace mantel to use on her Relationship Altar, which she would make in the coming week. She took the pieces of paper, placed them in the fireplace, and lit them. As the flames consumed the papers, she bowed her head and said a little prayer. "We offered our deepest desires to you tonight and surrendered them to the door of infinite possibility. Our hearts are pure and filled with gratitude. Thank you for your love, for great friendship, and for your presence in our lives." As the papers burned to ash she added, "We are so ready to meet the men of our dreams."

Sasha's Figurine on a Crescent Moon

She sat before the fire for a few more minutes, feeling content and expectant. Something old and outdated had been removed from her life; something vibrant and precious was sure to arrive. Faith felt it. She got up, stretched, and left the room as she hummed one of those "nice and flowy" songs, thinking about the single friends in her church group and how she couldn't wait to share with more of them what she'd been up to.

I have learned not to worry about love;

but to honor its coming with all my heart.

—ALICE WALKER

CHAPTER SIX

The Relationship Altar: Your Daily Connection to the Divine

Once a month you can approach your Full Moon Altar to give your intentions and your enthusiasm for life a terrific boost. On a daily basis, you can use your Relationship Altar to help you develop and maintain a strong connection with universal energy that will draw to you a meaningful relationship. Daily practice keeps your awareness focused on the subtle, more refined energies needed for attraction to occur. Your altar also will become your sanctuary.

The Benefits of Daily Practice

When you take time regularly to nourish your spirit, vitality and blessings follow. Whether your daily practice is meditation, prayer, chanting, Vedic breathing, spontaneous journaling—whatever you choose to do—when you do it in conjunction with your Relationship Altar it will help you attract Mr. Right. We heartily recommend beginning a daily practice, if you don't already have one. We like mornings the best, but any time is fine as long as it's daily.

Just as energy flowing unrestricted in your home and office supports you to receive more of what you want in life, so it is within the self. Directing your awareness inside regularly puts you in touch with the peace and contentment that naturally exist within each of us. When you find this place of inner calm, the world will reflect it back to you. You will draw to you what you desire.

The relationship you want receives support and strength when you open your heart to yourself and when you spend time before your altar.

Creating a Relationship Altar will help you with your practice by reminding you each time you see it of your heart's connection to your inner self, your intention, and your relationship with the divine. It is a conduit for positive energy to flow to you in miraculous ways and help you manifest your desires.

Action Step 4
Creating Your Relationship Altar

Place the altar in the northwest area of your home on a table, chest, windowsill, or other surface that will be undisturbed. If you have a missing northwest corner, or share a home with others and it is not convenient to have your altar in the northwest, it can be placed in the northwest area of a room, preferably on a *north* wall.

MICHAEL'S VASTU TIP: Facing north at your altar will support the concentration and focus you need for success.

Use a compass to make sure your altar is in the proper location.

SUGGESTIONS FOR YOUR RELATIONSHIP ALTAR

❁ Make sure the area you place your altar on is clean.

❁ Before you place the items on your altar, bathe and put on clean clothes.

❁ The surface you place your altar on should be easy to see as you sit in front of it, either on the floor or on a chair.

❁ Make sure that some of the pieces on the altar are *yellow* and *blue*.

PLACING THE ELEMENTS

❁ For the air element in the northwest, you can use small standing chimes, bird feathers, incense, a bird figurine, an angel, a fan, etc.

❁ For the water element in the northeast, use a cup or a bowl of water, a vase (either clear or translucent, in yellow or blue), or a small fountain. If you use a vase, you can add fresh or silk flowers to it. Make sure to keep the water fresh by changing it as needed.

Layout for the Relationship Altar

~ North~

NW			NE
a	p	w	
	o		
e		f	
SW			SE

a = Air

p = Personal Symbol

w = Water

o = Space

e = Earth

f = Fire

❀ Your earth element in the southwest can be a crystal, stones such as blue lace agate, or even pearls. You also can use a green plant or one that blooms with yellow or blue flowers, such as an African violet.

❀ In the southeast, a candle, or again incense, can be used to represent the fire element. Look for those that have the scent of ylang-ylang. It is associated with this altar. You also can use an oil lamp in this direction. Look for one that is silver in color or a plate that is silver, or has a silver finish, on which to place your candle.

❀ Your offering tray, which will go in the center of your altar, represents the space element and can be in the color, or combination of colors, of blue or yellow, silver-colored metal, or clear glass. Whatever you use, make it a complementary addition to your altar.

ADDITIONAL ITEMS FOR YOUR ALTAR

❀ Place your personal symbol in the center of your altar behind your offering tray. Many people use a statue to represent their heart's desires. Statues from the Vedic tradition include Parvati, who represents the supreme feminine energy or female power, and Krishna, who exemplifies loving relationships. You can create a collage made of old photographs, magazine clippings, or your own artwork. Add inspiring words and symbols to the collage, which can be framed in a silver-colored metal frame.

❀ To decorate your altar after you have the offering tray, element representations, and personal symbol in place, you can add a pair of items such as two small fish, two doves, two hearts—these represent loving relationships.

❉ To energize your altar, if you'd like, hang a blue crystal on a red string in increments of nine inches above the offering tray.

❉ Place the yantra you used for the Full Moon Altar on the offering tray for an added boost of cosmic energy.

❉ Other yantras can be added. They are available on the Web site in the resources section at the back of this book. You also could place Angel Cards® on your tray—whatever appeals to you and makes it beautiful and full of life.

❉ Remember: for the altar to work optimally for you, it must touch your heart, so take time to make it beautiful. When you appreciate your creation—when it delights you—your appreciation infuses it with loving energy, the same thing that you desire. By admiring your creation each time you look at it or sit in front of it, you receive that same energy back. Love and beauty make your heart light, joyous, and free.

IGNITING YOUR ALTAR: THE ENERGY BALL TECHNIQUE

You can ignite your altar with intention by using a technique that might seem a little strange but that is very effective. You make an energy vortex. Using this method, you draw energy with your hands and breath and "shape" it into a ball that energizes your altar. Here is the process.

❀ Stand or kneel in front of your completed altar and clear your mind by taking long, slow, deep breaths in through the nose and out through the mouth. As you exhale, make the sound *Ahhhh*. This will assist you in eliminating tension in the body.

❀ Bring your awareness to the feelings of fulfillment, love, and joy that you desire to experience in relationship with your Mr. Right.

❀ Hold your left hand in front of you at heart level, palm up.

❀ Take a deep breath in and, as you do so, bring your right arm straight up, palm extending toward the sky. As you slowly exhale, bring your right hand down toward the left palm. You will be creating an imaginary energy ball.

1. Hold your left hand in front of you at heart level, palm up.

2. Take a deep breath in and, as you do so, bring your right arm straight up, palm extending toward the sky.

3. As you slowly exhale, bring your right hand down toward the left palm.

4. After you have completed three rounds, transfer this imaginary ball into your right hand and place it over the top of your offering tray.

❋ Repeat this process three times. Each time you bring your right hand down toward your left, you will be able to feel the ball becoming more energized.

❋ After you have completed three rounds, transfer this imaginary ball into your right hand and place it over the top of your offering tray.

❋ You have created a vortex of energy filled with your dreams and desires. Your altar is now ignited.

You also can ignite your Relationship Altar with the Moon Yantra and Mantra used for the Full Moon Altar. Go to the Web site at *http://makingroomformrright.com/free yantra* to download the yantra and listen to the correct pronunciation of the mantra. Follow the activation ceremony instructions.

NICHOLE'S STORY

One of the women we worked with, Nichole, had a full life with more than enough work, a home she loved and tended with care, three cats, and wonderful friends. She had a home-based business and loved her life. The only thing lacking was a man. She hadn't had a date in three years. It didn't seem right that this beautiful, talented woman should be lacking the companionship she desired. She called me to see if there was something she could do to improve her prospects. She wasn't one to head for the local bars or grocery store aisles in hopes of finding her Mr. Right.

We talked about creating a Relationship Altar to attract a mate. I advised her of the layout and made suggestions of items to place on her altar. She created a beautiful, small altar in a garden window in her dining area. She carefully chose pieces that had significance to her—some crystals she had collected, precious items given to her by her mother, and a photo of good friends whose thirty-year marriage was still ripe with passion—and placed them lovingly on her altar. For her personal symbol she looked through a pile of magazines until she found the picture of a man with a warm smile and laughing eyes that touched her heart. She framed it and added it to her altar. We ignited the altar together, and within less than a month she had three interesting men all vying for her time and attention. She chose the one with gentle ways and a giving heart.

Ask for what you want! Be clear about the feelings you wish in your life, and focus only on those. Don't focus on the nuances of how they will occur, when they will happen, who Mr. Right will be, etc. Those are not feelings but thoughts that will trap your mind. You will never find your Mr. Right this way. In surrendering your heart's desires to the divine you allow the universe to present you with its gifts.

Take time each day for you. Look forward to your practice, whether it's in the morning, afternoon, or evening. It is your ally in your quest for Mr. Right. Taking the time for yourself to build your spiritual connection with the divine brings peace, contentment, and possibility into your life.

Wake each morning with a smile and a prayer! Being happy is a choice. Set the tone of your day by waking each morning and bringing a smile to your face, and a prayer for this and every day to be filled with gratitude and grace.

Sasha, Faith, and Lori are preparing their Relationship Altars. Let's see how they are doing.

Relationship Altars for Transformation

LORI

For privacy, and because she had the perfect location for it, Lori decided to create the Relationship Altar in her bedroom under a large picture window that looked out to the backyard. She placed the altar on an old hope chest that was her grandmother's. There was more than enough room in front of it to sit in meditation or do yoga.

She'd carefully gathered items for her altar, visiting secondhand stores and a few antique stores, as well as local gift stores, looking for the perfect pieces. She ordered a few items online: a statue of Parvati that attracted her as her personal symbol, and two copper yantras to place on her offering tray.

Lori had covered the top of the chest with a colorful scarf she rarely wore but loved. It was painted in blues and yellows. She added other elements: a group of feathers in a small container collected on walks near the lake for the air element in the northwest; a crystal vase filled with purified water and yellow roses as the water element in the northeast; two candles in shades of blue symbolizing her and her mate-to-be, placed on a decorative yellow plate to represent fire in the southeast; and a potted jasmine plant in the southwest for earth. Lori's offering tray, in the center of the altar, was a silver candy dish that belonged to her mother. As a final touch, she added the statue of Parvati. When Lori stepped back to look at what she had created, she was pleased. She then added the two copper yantras to her offering tray. One represented Ganesh, the remover of obstacles, and the other represented Lakshmi, the goddess of prosperity, peace, abundance, and harmony. Lori also placed a pair of small porcelain doves, again symbolizing her and her mate, in front of the potted jasmine plant. Finally she added small, pretty stones of lapis and yellow agate from her collection of crystals and stones on the tray.

Just as she was admiring her work, her daughter Emma walked in to ask her a question. Emma stopped, surprised at what she saw by the window. "It's beautiful," Emma said, stepping closer to examine the altar. "So this is what you've been collecting things for. *Mmmm* . . . now I get it!"

"I had no idea how pretty it would be," Lori said, surprised at the beauty of her own creation, "until I put it all together." The two of them stood there, arm in arm, admiring the altar, mesmerized by it.

"It really is beautiful, Mom. You did a great job." Emma gave Lori a hug.

Lori then decided to call Faith to tell her about the altar. "It has real presence," Lori told her. "You should come see it." Faith, who was just stepping out for a walk, said she would be right over.

When she arrived, for several minutes the two women gazed at the altar in silence. "I see what you mean," Faith admitted. "It definitely has presence."

"Let's hope it brings presents!" Lori joked. "But really, I hope it turns the energy up a bit."

"Haven't you felt some changes already? I have." Faith turned to look at her friend.

"Well, come to think of it, I've noticed a few men catch my eye and smile or talk to me, sort of flirtatiously, which hasn't happened in a long time. You know, I hadn't put two and two together. This must be working!"

FAITH

Faith had experienced her own changes. She had been feeling positive about life in general and felt an energetic boost from the full moon evening they had together. She had shared her experience with her church group, and several of the women had voiced interest in learning more about what she was up to. She also had met a nice-looking man who was out walking his little Shih Tzu. Being an animal lover,

Faith had stopped to pet the dog and had a conversation with its owner, Chris. She had run into him almost every day after that, as they walked at the same time. She swore he was flirting with her, and she thought it was fun.

Lori could tell that Faith was feeling really good, and her acquaintance with Chris added some sparkle to her whole being. "Let's keep checking in with each other," she told Faith, "to keep up with the changes, so we'll know this is working."

"Absolutely," Faith agreed. "We'll be witnesses of each other's transformation—that will help keep it real."

IGNITING LORI'S ALTAR

Together that afternoon they ignited Lori's altar. They sat and did the breathing exercise they had been using since they had written their lists for the Full Moon Altar evening. Then Lori used her imagination to feel what she might feel if she were in a relationship with that special man. She then began the Energy Ball Technique: she brought her left hand to her heart, palm up, and raised her right arm straight up as she took a deep breath in. As she exhaled, she brought her right hand down over her left and began to focus on the energy she built in her hands. She felt a vibrating sensation in the palms of her hands.

Lori then inhaled and exhaled two more times. She brought her right hand down to form the energy ball; each time she felt the ball become denser and more real. After the third round of up and down, she brought her left hand over her right, transferred the ball into her right hand, and placed it on the offering tray in the center of her altar.

She sat for a moment quietly, recalling how the energy had felt in her hands and gazing at the altar, which seemed alive with the energy.

"I felt the energy build as I brought my right hand down when I exhaled," she said as she turned and looked at Faith, whose eyes were closed. Faith had a dreamy look on her face even as she slowly opened her eyes.

"Well, I enjoyed this immensely," Faith said, feeling serene. Her face looked relaxed and soft. "I just kept feeling a lot of love for you. It was powerful and peaceful at the same time." She got up from her seat on the floor. "I know it's going to draw a wonderful man into your life. I can feel it." She gave Lori a big hug. "Let's talk later. I'm so inspired I want to get back and put my altar together."

SASHA

Sasha had put her Relationship Altar together with items she had been collecting for years and had saved from her clutter-clearing. She found it really difficult to decide which ones to use, then finally realized that she could change items over time whenever she felt like it. Sasha's altar was simple and lovely. Each of the items representing the elements held special meaning for her. She knew something significant was happening when she looked at her altar, after placing everything in its proper place, and she felt her spirits lift. She also knew that by simply sitting before it every day—which might be the only practice she did—and saying a prayer or thinking about what she wanted, she had faith that a great relationship would manifest in her life. After all the good changes that had happened for her since beginning Vastu, she believed in its effectiveness.

She had especially felt change in the air since the Full Moon Altar evening. She mentioned this to her assistant, Corrine, who had been receptive. Corrine had been single longer than she cared to admit. Not only did Vastu sound like a fun way to spend time with friends, it also appealed to her adventurous side. She wanted to know more about what Sasha was doing.

MICHAEL'S VASTU TIP: If you are a collector of things such as seashells, bird feathers, interesting stones, or any kind of trinkets, these items make great additions to an altar. Make an altar that touches your heart by placing things you care about on it. And it's fine to change items from time to time as long as the basic layout remains the same.

FAITH

Faith's altar was a work of love. After she came home from Lori's, Faith was so inspired that she created her altar, then sat down and did the ignition process. She sat for meditation for ten minutes, and after she was done, opened her eyes and gazed at the altar, admiring the candle flame and relishing the beauty of her creation. She was pleased with the items she had chosen. It seemed that each one was a perfect choice for this altar. She had used one of her mother's many crocheted doilies on top of a table that had once had piles of papers and books on it. It now was the perfect location for her Relationship Altar.

She reflected on the past few weeks and how since the full moon evening she had felt lighter—like something old had been taken away. She now felt a level of optimism and contentment that was so different from anything she had experienced before. She thought about Chris, the man she met walking in the neighborhood. He'd been living there for years, walking his dog in the park across from her house—right under her nose! Funny how they had never met until now. He had called her to ask her to dinner. She thought about it: that extra boost of cosmic energy, and voilà!—a phone call and a date. She truly looked forward to the next technique that Lori had promised to tell her and Sasha about. Faith was enjoying the feeling of living with an open heart.

Since love grows within you, so beauty grows.

For love is the beauty of the soul.

—ST. AUGUSTINE

CHAPTER SEVEN

Yantras and Mantras: Tools of Attraction

When the insightful sages thousands of years ago developed the technology of Vastu, they included the science of yantras and mantras. These two tools attract and enhance whatever is desirable—including, of course, a great relationship.

It may seem strange in this age of computers and electronics that what appears to be a simple drawing on a page can help you get what you need and want—from improved health, to prosperity, to business success, to spiritual upliftment, to love—but yantras can and do. These energetic devices and their corresponding sounds (mantras) dynamically and effectively saturate the environment with sound frequencies that draw to the diligent practitioner the support needed for fulfillment.

Sound and Scientific Discoveries

More than forty years ago, a Swiss doctor, researcher, and artist named Hans Jenny invented an apparatus called a Tonoscope, which he used to demonstrate the direct correlation between sound and form. As he spoke many different sounds into a microphone, distinct shapes would form on the surface of the Tonoscope for each sound. When *Om*, the universal mantra, which represents the manifest and unmanifest aspects of God, or the divine, is spoken into the Tonoscope microphone, it generates a circle with various triangular shapes. This form is the same one that the Vedic sages used. They called it the Shree Yantra and considered it to be the most powerful yantra for positive outcomes in all of life's ventures.

The Vedic seers weren't alone in their recognition of the power of sound. Many spiritual traditions speak of it. The Bible says, "In the beginning there was the word . . ." Buddhism, Hinduism, and other traditions consider singing or chanting to be a viable and powerful way to communicate with the divine. The Vedas tell us that the five elements—

earth, air, fire, water, and space—originated from the sound *Om*, the seed of existence and the material world.

Just as names connect us to people and places, so sounds link us to the unseen. Mantras and yantras communicate our feelings and intentions to invisible forces that manifest what may seem like miracles. From a Vedic perspective, however, and even from a quantum physics perspective, the miracles are natural occurrences created by the intelligent use of energy.

Quantum physics tells us that everything is energy vibrating at different frequencies. Our thoughts, hopes, and desires, as well as our feelings, emanate from our energetic fields as electromagnetic vibrations. These vibrations create our destiny. It is vitally important to be aware of how we are feeling, what we are thinking and desiring, because the frequencies of, for example, sadness and disappointment add extra power to our thoughts—they tinge whatever we think about ourselves and everything else.

You've probably noticed that when you are unhappy or depressed, your whole body feels heavy, almost weighted down, and your mood feels heavy, too. When feelings such as these go unchecked, their associated negative frequencies strengthen, become your status quo, and go with you into the future. They draw to you more of the same.

Yantras and mantras can balance your energy and elevate

heavier energetic frequencies, moving you to a lighter, happier experience. Over time, the regular use of mantras and yantras will shift any negative frequencies you have (experienced as negative beliefs about your self-worth, for example, or repetitive, unproductive thoughts, etc.) and produce an ongoing positive state of being. When performed daily, this system of personal transformation, like nothing else we've seen, moves you forward into a life of fulfillment and joy.

Action Step 5
Using Sound and Form to Attract Relationships

Before you actually use a yantra, it has to be energized, which we'll show you how to do. It takes only a few minutes.

FIRST THINGS FIRST

We suggest that you choose two yantras to begin. Use them and their associated mantras on your Relationship Altar for forty days and observe during that time the effect they have on your life. If after forty days you'd like to experience the influence of another yantra or two, remove the two you have worked with and replace them with the new ones. It is fine to place the yantras you are not working with on your altar, but not on your offering tray. Only place the yantras you are working with on your offering tray. You will chant the corresponding mantras and do the daily energizing ceremony only with the two yantras you are working with.

MICHAEL'S VASTU TIP: All yantras have power and can create change in your life. By using only one or two at a time, you will be able to specifically tell which yantra is influencing the change in your life.

RELATIONSHIP YANTRAS AND MANTRAS: PREPARATION FOR USE

If you have already made your Relationship Altar, you may have other objects representing the elements, but for this process you specifically need rice, accessible water, a candle, incense, and a bell. Place these additional representations of the elements next to the ones you already have. They do not need to be duplicated if you are already using them as symbols on your altar.

> *Earth*—rice in a small bowl in the southwest
>
> *Water*—purified water in a small cup in the north east

Fire—a small candle in the southeast

Air—incense in an easy-to-manage incense holder in the northwest

Space—a small bell placed directly behind your offering tray.

Before beginning, as with all ceremonies and practices, we suggest that you bathe and put on clean clothes.

To begin, place one of the yantras in the middle of your offering tray.

MICHAEL'S VASTU TIP: Have the second yantra near your altar, but not on the altar directly, until it is time to activate it. Then add it to your offering tray.

ACTIVATING YOUR RELATIONSHIP YANTRAS

Take a moment to set your intention for fulfillment of your desire: attracting Mr. Right. Take a few long, slow breaths in through the nose and out through the mouth. Then begin the process as described on the next few pages, starting with the earth element.

Earth Element

Pick up the bowl containing the rice with your left hand and move it in a slow, clockwise motion *one time* as you chant the mantra synchronized with the clockwise motion. Do this motion one more time, accompanied with chanting the mantra one more time. Then place the bowl of rice down.

Water Element

Pick up the cup of water representing the water element with the left hand and go through the same clockwise motion synchronized with the chanting of the mantra *twice* through.

Fire Element

Now do the same process with the candle, which represents the fire element. Chant the mantra synchronized with the clockwise motion of the candle *twice* through.

Air Element

Do this process with the incense, representing the air element, *twice* through as well.

Space Element

Finally, for the space element, pick up the bell and ring it three times as you chant the mantra—but chant it only *once* through.

When you have completed this process you will have chanted the mantra a total of nine times to activate the yantra. Additionally, if you wish, you may continue to chant the mantra while sitting quietly in front of your altar in increments of 9 times up to 108 times each day. It takes about five minutes, maximum, to chant each mantra 108 times.

MANTRA BEAD NECKLACES

To keep track of the number of repetitions, you can use a mantra bead necklace, or *mala*. This is a tool, similar to a rosary, that supports chanting and meditation practices. Consisting of 108 beads each, malas are made of different stones or woods. We prefer sandalwood, semi-precious stones, or Rudrak-

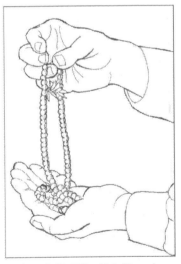

How to Hold the Mala Properly

sha beads, which are the seeds of a tree that is sacred in India and which are said to have healing properties. Each of these types of malas holds mantra vibrations particularly well.

To use your mala, hold it in the right hand between the thumb and middle finger. After each mantra repetition, touch the next bead until you have touched all 108 beads. Wearing your mala after chanting ensures that the vibrations of the chant continue to uplift you.

RELATIONSHIP YANTRAS AND MANTRAS: TOOLS OF TRANSFORMATION

These yantras encourage relationships. We say "encourage" because love can never be forced into being. As you put Vastu techniques into practice, you will understand more deeply the principle of attraction, as opposed to grabbing hold of, chasing, or forcing. You will feel more and more that you have unlimited support flowing to you from the universal source and that you don't have to make yourself crazy trying.

To assist you, we've created a Web page where you can download free versions of yantras and hear the mantras chanted. To access this page, go to *http://www.makingroom formrright.com/freeyantra*.

THE MOON YANTRA

Just as you used the Moon Yantra to activate the Full Moon Altar, you can use it on your Relationship Altar to support the fulfillment of your heart's desires. This beautiful yantra attracts positive relationships, aids in successful communication, and helps draw to you your heart's desires.

Mantra:
Om Namo Bhagavate Vasudevaya Namaha

Phonetic pronunciation:
Om Na-mo Ba-ga-va-tay Va-su-day-vai-ya Na-ma-ha

Moon Yantra

VASHI KARAN YANTRA

The Vashi Karan Yantra is used specifically to attract a mate. When combined in a regular practice with its associated mantra, it also creates harmony and enhances existing relationships.

Mantra:
Om Shree Devadantamay Vashankuru Namaha

Phonetic pronunciation:
Om Shree-Deva-danta-mayaa-Vashan-kuru Na-ma-ha

Vashi Karan Yantra

VENUS YANTRA

The Venus Yantra bestows respect, love, and peace of mind.

It is associated with fire, passion, love, and attraction, including sexual energy—all absolutely essential for a relationship.

Mantra:

Om Namo Bhagavate Parasuramaya Namaha

Phonetic pronunciation:

Om Na-mo Ba-ga-va-tay Para-sura-mai-ya Na-ma-ha

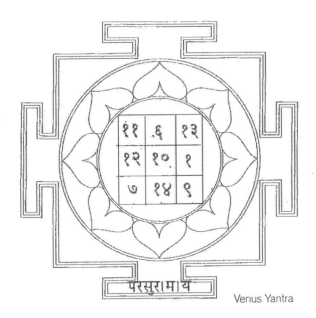

Venus Yantra

KAMDEV YANTRA

This yantra is a powerful ally in attracting someone to love; it enlivens sexual energy.

Mantra:

Om Klim Kamdev Namaha

Phonetic pronunciation:

Om K-lim Kaam-dev Na-ma-ha

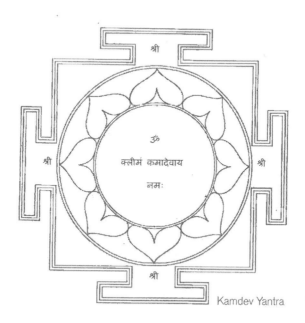

Kamdev Yantra

Being respectful and sincere. Daily practice of mantra recital will influence your life in a myriad of ways. When you respect the power of this process and are sincere in your commitment to yourself, you will reap incredible rewards.

Have patience—you're worth it! Your life is changing; you are evolving into the person you have always wanted to be. Patience is key. Allow the process to unfold. Don't push.

Love your commitments. Look forward to your practice each day. Know that you are stimulating the energetic center that is the source of your future. From this center, what is yet to come will manifest. Bless yourself, have compassion for any resistance, and honor your commitment to making room for Mr. Right!

Lori, Faith, and Sasha are beginning to explore yantras and mantras. Lori has started to share her experiences with another friend, too. Let's see how the three friends are doing.

How Sound and Form Create Change

The three women have committed to spending time each morning in front of their Relationship Altars chanting the mantras they have chosen and doing their regular spiritual practices. Lori, more disciplined than Faith or Sasha in spiritual commitment, looked forward to daily yoga practice at the crack of dawn and sitting afterward for meditation. She found that adding mantras to her early-morning routine created extra energy and focus.

By the third day of chanting after yoga, Lori felt comfortable enough with the pronunciation of the mantras and the activation process of the yantras to do additional chanting using her sandalwood mantra bead necklace. She liked quietly chanting aloud, and after she finished chanting the mantra for the second yantra 108 times, she sat with her spine erect to meditate. Within the stillness after chanting she noticed that energy was coursing through her body. She felt incredibly alive and vibrant. She remembered that she had read about the power of Sanskrit, which is the language of the mantras. Each syllable of Sanskrit, the sages said, carries the power of the life force itself. Based on her experience, Lori believed it.

MICHAEL'S VASTU TIP: If you choose to chant the mantras within the mind instead of verbalizing them, chant the mantra once out loud. This can be done quietly. Never chant the word *Om* within the mind, as it creates a more reclusive energy—not one you want for finding the man of your dreams. Therefore drop the *Om* altogether if you are chanting the mantra within the mind.

At work later that day, Lori ran into her friend Charlene in the hospital cafeteria. Charlene, a beautiful African American woman and the director of personnel for the hospital, considered herself an astute judge of what was happening with her friends. Her antennae focused on Lori. Charlene took a closer look and noticed that Lori looked radiant. "Is there a new man in your life?" Charlene asked as she stepped closer, curious. "I swear I haven't seen you glowing like this ever, girl. What are you doing with yourself? *Hmmm?*"

Lori laughed and gave her a hug. It was Charlene who had interviewed Lori for her first job at the hospital years before. They became good friends, sharing kid stories and complaints about their workaholic husbands. "You would never believe it, if I told you," Lori said with a twinkle in her eyes. "But I'll show you. Why don't you come over after work for tea and we'll talk. I think you might find what I'm doing right up your alley, so to speak."

"How could I resist?" Charlene said, intrigued. "I'll be there as soon as I can after work. See you then." She walked back to her office thinking about her friend and all they'd been through.

With three boys; Daniel, her husband, a corporate lawyer; and work commitments; Charlene's life was full. She wanted to find a way to put some sparkle back into her marriage. She felt if she had that, she'd be on top of the world. As she turned into Lori's street, she thought, *That girl's up to something or I don't know my Lori. I can't wait to find out what she's got going on.*

Moments later, Charlene was sitting on the floor of Lori's bedroom listening to Lori explain about the nuances of Vastu, from clearing clutter to creating the Relationship Altar.

"Wow," Charlene said after hearing about the Full Moon Altar. Looking at the altar in front of them and back at Lori, Charlene saw the change in her that was not physical but radiating from within her. "Now tell me what else you are doing, because there is definitely something happening here that I want to be part of. You know what I mean?"

Like Lori, you might find that others sense the changes within you, too. "Isn't it interesting, Charlene? You can feel it, can't you?" Lori said. "Something is definitely happening. There's some greater force at play that is affecting me energetically. It clicked in after we did the Full Moon Altar together, and it got stronger after I ignited the Relationship Altar and began chanting the mantras."

"Okay, you lost me. What chanting? What mantras? You are way over my head here," Charlene said, laughing.

Lori told Charlene about the use of mantras and yantras and the layout so Charlene could put together a Relationship Altar. She also invited her to the next Full Moon Altar Ceremony.

Charlene was touched by Lori's generosity of spirit and thanked her for caring enough to share everything with her. After giving her old friend a hug, Lori looked into Charlene's eyes, seeing herself mirrored there. "I just want to see you happy and content, Charlene. It's what I want for all my friends . . . it's what I want for the world. I think this work has power and meaning beyond what we can intellectually understand. This may sound, I don't know, grandiose, but more and more I think this is a wonderful opportunity for women, and men, to get together in a brand-new way. I think even Daniel will appreciate this once he sees how it affects you. And the boys will, too."

"*Hmmm*, well, we'll see about that," Charlene replied, thinking of her boys and husband.

"I'll bet they'll be interested," Lori said enthusiastically. "There's a lot of heart in this, and doing it with Faith and Sasha and now sharing it with you makes me see how it can bring people together. It's made me aware of how we're all connected anyway, and being conscious of that is so fulfilling. I'd love to experience more community, and I think this might be a key to creating it. It can change our lives and open us to more loving relationships with men and women, too."

"I understand what you're saying," Charlene said with a sigh. "It's like even though I have a family, I feel isolated sometimes and really, really need my women friends."

"Well, we're here for you," Lori said smiling, giving her a hug.

Charlene thanked Lori for the information and inspiration. Feeling a bit of a buzz, Charlene drove home knowing she was ready for change, and committed to finding out more about Vastu and how it could help her find a new way.

FAITH

Sasha called Faith to check in and found her friend happy and full of energy. Faith told her she was chanting and beginning to feel like a man-magnet. While she giggled at the response, Sasha asked her if men were uncontrollably being drawn to her. Faith felt all the attention from men was a result of her new practices. She told Sasha about the cute contractor doing some remodeling at her next-door neighbor's house. She said he was younger than she. "He's either flirting with me or one of the nicest guys around," she said. She also mentioned her walking partner,

Chris, whom she was enjoying getting to know immensely.

Finally there was her newest man friend, Avery, who owned a new restaurant in town. She had gone to his restaurant a few times when she needed to get away from the house. Working and living in the same place got to her sometimes, so she took walking breaks. She found his restaurant, became kind of a regular, and one day he sat down with her. Now every time she went in, he'd talk with her over tea or food, and they'd have wonderful, esoteric conversations. She found out he was a widower; she wanted him to ask her out for a more "serious" date.

Faith saw the shift in her life in a short time. The new order in her home felt good and added to a sense of expanded possibilities she hadn't felt in a long time. With the walking she was doing, her aches and pains were not the first things she thought about when she got out of bed in the morning. She didn't feel as easily frustrated and was sleeping better, even with the seasons changing. Her mood was upbeat.

She had thought she needed a man to be happy, but what Faith found was she really needed herself. She enjoyed being single this way and liked the male attention. It was good for her heart to be open and welcoming, and not feel that she had to fall for a man just because he appeared to be interested in her. This was very freeing for her.

SASHA

Sasha had met a man, too—the man at the antique store where she had taken her Deco treasures after de-cluttering. Periodically she had gone into the shop to see how things were selling and to create little displays in the store windows or in cabinets inside the store to show off her pieces better. She had thought that the man, whose name was Elliott, was annoyed with her because he watched her intensely every time she came in. She didn't realize he was as shy as she.

One evening several days after the Full Moon Altar event at Faith's house, Sasha rushed to the antique shop after work. She tripped and fell as she entered the store, hitting her head. As she related the incident to Faith, "The next thing I knew Elliott was holding my head in his lap, and he had a piece of wet paper towel over a lump on my forehead. I was a little dazed. He was being very patient and sweet, stroking my hair. It was the first time anyone has held me in a long time." Sasha remembered feeling surprised that it felt so comforting and good to be held by a man. "He was so tender with me. Something just happened . . . he bent down and kissed me, on the lips, gently. I think he felt embarrassed that he did it, but when he began to pull away, I threw my arms around his neck and kissed him back!"

That moment of action and response changed Sasha's life.

It marked the ending of the self-imposed moratorium on intimacy she had set so firmly in place. It opened her to feelings of need, passion, and desire that she had repressed, even claimed were insignificant, for so long. If she had thought about what she was doing, her actions would have shocked her, but there was an energy compelling her forward, willing her to keep her guard down and explore the emotional terrain that felt foreign yet demanded her attention.

When the three friends had dinner together later and Lori heard Faith and Sasha's updates, Lori felt affirmed in everything she was doing and happy for both of them. She heard the freedom and happiness in Faith's voice and the excitement and anticipation, plus a large dose of willingness to embrace whatever came next, in Sasha's.

"It really feels like a floodgate has opened—I'm ready to open up my heart," Sasha said in amazement. She told her friends about how honest, open, and gentle Elliott was with her.

"Weren't those the qualities you asked for at the Full Moon Ceremony, Sasha?" Faith sat back in her chair, remembering Sasha's words.

"You're right! Oh my God! I didn't stop to think about the lists and those three words. Okay, I give up, you guys.

This stuff really is working." She sat back in her chair, realizing that she had created this. "He was there all along and I didn't see it, or couldn't see it. Maybe I was just too afraid to see what was possible. Wow!"

"Keep embracing the love, Sasha." Lori leaned over and gave Sasha's hand a squeeze. "Just focus on what you do want with Elliott, and don't let fear or the past bring your energy down. If you keep your intention focused on the positive and know you have a right to happiness, the doors will continue to open."

Faith chimed in, "Lori, I just want to say—the Vastu work we've done, the Vedic mantras, actually all the stuff you've shared with us so far has been amazingly helpful. Thank you for opening us up to this knowledge."

Sasha agreed enthusiastically.

"It works best when there is curiosity and desire for change," Lori replied. "Vastu enhances our attunement with our highest good, the highest intention of spirit. All the Vedic practices in the world won't work if your mind is closed and full of judgment and negativity. We just need to applaud ourselves for being willing and for the strength of our desire to remain open."

Lori suggested that they continue to work on their chanting because there were more Vastu tips she wanted to share with them to boost the positive energy in them and in their surroundings. "I have some fine-tuning ideas for the home," she said, then added with a smile, "including the bedroom."

"I can't wait," Sasha said with a grin. "Would you all mind if I invite Corrine to one of our meetings about Vastu? I think she would really like it."

Lori smiled. "Sure. I don't mind. I'd like to invite Charlene, too."

"Well then," Faith added, filled with the vision of expanding their Vastu community, "I have a couple of women from my church who are interested. I'll ask them, too."

The three women said their good-byes, relishing the possibility of more of something they never thought they'd welcome: change.

The only things in life you regret

are the risks you didn't take.

—Anonymous

CHAPTER EIGHT

Enhance Your Environment Through Color, Crystals, Gems, and Scent

Just as sound or mantra can be used to attract a relationship, certain colors, crystals, gems, stones, and scents can enhance the energy in your physical surroundings. When used with awareness, they act as attractors and will help draw to you a relationship with Mr. Right. Wearing scents and gems or stones also affects you in a positive way.

Many of the recommendations we're offering here not only enhance your power to attract, they also help you create a kinder relationship within yourself. Fostering love of self is essential for attracting the love you wish to receive from another. Anxiety, depression, and low self-esteem undermine attempts to find deeper love with the man of your dreams. Therefore, we encourage you to explore these beautiful, natural tools.

At the end of this chapter you'll be introduced to several tips for fine-tuning your bedroom so you will get the rest you need. Without a good night's sleep in a calm and peaceful haven of retreat, it is difficult to experience the grace and ease you need during the day. Relationships suffer as tiredness and stress reduce your ability to be open and available to intimacy.

Action Step 6
Implementing Fine-Tuning Suggestions: Putting Them to Work for You

To infuse your home and your life with the energies of peace, well-being, attraction, and love, add one or two of the following suggestions at a time. Give yourself time to sense the impact of each one.

THE COLORS OF PASSION FOR YOUR BEDROOM

Color can influence your life in positive ways. It can be used to create ambience in the bedroom and bring passion into your life. All shades of red, from the darkest of reds and burgundies to the lightest of pinks, have a stimulating influence on your love life.

The wavelength for the color red is the longest in the color spectrum and has the lowest frequency. It fires up your physiology and produces qualities of strength, courage, and steadfastness. Red increases enthusiasm and stimulates energy. It enlivens the base chakra, which is related to passion and sexuality.

MICHAEL'S VASTU TIP: A word of caution here: a little goes a long way. Red is extremely stimulating.

According to Vastu, if your bedroom is in the south, red can be used in the color of cushions, a bedspread, or wall hangings, as it is considered a primary color for this area. In the southeast red can be used without causing overstimulation, although use it less than in the south, keeping it to a secondary color. In the southwest, use more earthy tones of red, moving toward deeper oranges and browns.

But if your bedroom is in another area of your home (west, northwest, north, northeast, or east), use red only as an accent color, such as in throw pillows, or use it for a small enhancement color in a pattern for curtains. Don't ever use it as a wall color or a bedspread.

Lingerie in reds or pink is considered very seductive. Adding cut flowers or scented candles in reds in your bedroom adds warmth and sensuality, and is another way to use red as an accent color.

Pink is a toned-down version of red and can be used in any direction. Pink has a tranquil and calming influence on the nervous system. A mixture of red and white, it is soothing to anxious or aggressive behavior. The white in pink raises the frequency of red and has a purifying and healing influence in the environment. You can use pink as an accent color, as it adds grace, happiness, refinement, and joy to your bedroom. Bedsheets and pillowcases in pink are a wonderful way to experience this color. Pink candles and flowers are wonderful accents, too.

CRYSTALS THAT IMPROVE THE AMBIENCE OF YOUR HOME

Faceted hanging crystal balls are not only beautiful to look at, they also are effective in balancing and enhancing the energy in any room in your home, making it more welcoming and inviting. If you have a sharp corner projecting into a room, a hanging crystal can be used to soften it. These corners are areas where environmental stress collects, causing an uneasy feeling in the room. This uneasiness plays on your mind, and you may find yourself cycling through past thoughts and experiences that are held by this stress.

To eliminate the influence, hang a twenty-millimeter or thirty-millimeter clear, faceted, leaded crystal ball on a red string, in increments of nine inches long, in front of the projection. It will keep the energy moving and will reduce the tension in the room.

You also can hang a twenty-millimeter blue crystal in the northwest corner of your bedroom to stimulate the energy of relationships there, or hang a blue crystal over the offering tray of your Relationship Altar to keep the energy moving toward manifesting your dreams. Again, hang the crystal in increments of nine inches on a red string or thread.

MICHAEL'S VASTU TIP: Clean your crystals monthly, using purified water; allow them to air-dry on a clean towel. Do not use a crystal that has been damaged or chipped. It will not be as effective.

GEMS THAT ENHANCE LOVING RELATIONSHIPS

There are specific gems and stones that balance and support loving relationships, especially between you and Mr. Right. Some of the more common stones can be placed in the bedroom, in a small decorative bowl or in a saucer on your nightstand by the bed. You can create a collection of a variety of complementary stones, too. Stones can be purchased as larger pieces for display, or they can be worn as beads in a necklace, bracelet, or ring and kept on your Relationship Altar in your offering tray when you are not wearing them.

Rose quartz promotes romantic love as well as self-love and acceptance. It is the stone of forgiveness, humility, and patience. It teaches us to open our hearts and to be tender, peaceful, and gentle. This is a fairly inexpensive stone and can be worn as a bracelet or a necklace. When not being worn, place rose quartz by your bed for peace and serenity, or add it to your offering tray on your Relationship Altar. Tuck a piece of tumbled rose quartz into each of the four corners of your bedroom to encourage loving relationships in your life.

The luminous ruby is associated with romantic love and love of self. This is a precious stone and can be expensive.

Ruby brings integrity, devotion, and happiness. It is said to strengthen both the physical and the emotional heart, bringing courage to the wearer. Confidence, vitality, stamina, and strength are all qualities associated with ruby. Rose quartz and garnet are less expensive choices for receiving the benefits inherent in ruby.

Moonstone holds protective energy and is balancing for the emotions. Like rose quartz, moonstone is not an expensive stone. It is known to attract love and affection, and when placed under the pillow at night it supports peaceful sleep.

Blue lace agate brings calming energy to a hectic life. It has a healing energy, strengthens intuition and inspiration, enhances communication, and combats envy and spite. It promotes love of self and understanding. This stone is reasonably priced and easily available. Blue lace agates can be beautiful, decorative additions to a Relationship Altar, and as tumbled stones are not expensive.

Lemon quartz is said to alleviate negative patterns. It also helps with communication, lifts your spirit, and spreads positive feelings. Prices for this stone vary, depending on its quality.

Amethyst enhances peace, understanding, and humility. It brings contentment, healing, happiness, and love. The larger stones can be placed on your altar. Wearing this beautiful purple stone calms the mind and opens the heart. Pricing depends on the quality of the stone and whether it is for wear or display.

Pearl signifies purity and beauty, compassion, protection, and love. When used as jewelry it has a soothing influence on the body. It is advisable to wear natural, not man-made pearls. Natural pearls are more expensive than man-made pearls, and prices vary dramatically, depending on the quality.

Garnet is known to stimulate sex drive, improve feminine sensuality, and combat depression. Its fiery red shade is said to be symbolic of passion, inspiration, love, and romance. Wear it as a necklace or add pieces of tumbled stones to the offering tray of your Relationship Altar. Prices for these stones vary, depending on quality. You can get tumbled stones to add to your altar for much less than the price of faceted jewelry-quality stones.

Kunzite supports calm and balance, and enhances good fortune and spiritual equilibrium. It is the stone for finding true love, harmony, compassion, and inner peace. Add a piece to your offering tray and carry a piece of it in your pocket. Kunzite is not an inexpensive stone even uncut, but it is indeed beautiful and worth exploring if your budget permits it.

Green jade is considered one of the most precious stones of the East. It strengthens love and happiness and fortifies the physical body. It is a stone of the heart, both physically and emotionally. It is said to fulfill dreams and encourage long life. Jade can be worn as rings, pendants, and bracelets, or it can be placed on your altar in a variety of shapes, from the shape of an egg, to spheres, to carved as animals or Buddha. Prices vary, depending on the quality of the stone.

SCENTS THAT SUPPORT BALANCE, LOVE, AND WELL-BEING

Essential oils are beneficial for supporting self-love, acceptance, and sensuality. Used for thousands of years for their medicinal and aromatic purposes, the oils we recommend are to enhance relationships, with others as well as yourself. These scents stimulate the connection between the emotions and the mind, and open you to experience higher levels of consciousness.

Oils are valued for their therapeutic properties as well as their fragrance. When inhaled, oils penetrate into areas of the brain, oxygenating the whole body, including the limbic region of the brain, which is the seat of emotions, intuition, and sex drive. This system connects to parts of the brain that control heart rate, breathing rate, blood pressure, and stress levels. To say that essential oils can mollify stress levels is an understatement. Additionally, your sense of smell is connected to your hormonal system, which impacts how you think, feel, and perceive yourself in your daily life.

You can diffuse oils in a vaporizer, or they can be gently heated to release the scent into the air. They can be added to bathwater, massage oil, or unscented body lotion. You can use essential oils as you would perfume. You even can make up a mixture of purified water and a few drops of essential oil and spray it on your sheets.

Lavender is known to balance the body by promoting higher states of consciousness, health, love, and peace. It enhances a sense of well-being.

Ylang-ylang oil is an aphrodisiac and has euphoric properties. It supports emotional balance, influences sexual energy, and enhances relationships. This oil encourages feelings of confidence, joy, self-love and acceptance, and peace.

Juniper enhances emotional balance and evokes feelings of love and peace while it elevates spiritual awareness.

Patchouli is sedating, calming, and relaxing, and helps reduce anxiety. It may have some influence on sexual and physical energy.

Bergamot relieves anxiety, depression, nervous tension, and stress. It is known to support emotional balance. Bergamot provides an emotional boost and encouragement. It can be successfully blended with the oils of sandalwood, lavender, and ylang-ylang, and applied to the inside crease of your elbow to stabilize the emotions.

Rose is stimulating and elevating to the mind, as it creates a sense of well-being. Its fragrance is almost intoxicating and aphrodisiac-like. The heart-opening fragrance of rose combats hormonal stress, postnatal depression, and stress following the breakdown of emotional relationships.

Neroli is calming and relaxing to the body and spirit. It strengthens and stabilizes the emotions and encourages confidence, courage, joy, peace, and sensuality. It helps us to see what is beautiful in life.

Jasmine is known in India as the "queen of the night" and "moonlight of the grove." Women have treasured it for centuries for its beautiful, aphrodisiac-like fragrance. A symbol in many traditions of hope, happiness, and love, its scent uplifts the emotions and promotes powerful, inspirational relationships. Jasmine traditionally is used as a fertility herb. It is stimulating and has antidepressant qualities. In India, women use this oil in their hair at night so their husbands will be drawn to them.

Rosewood is calming to the mind and relaxing to the body. Its fragrance enhances feelings of peace and gentleness.

Geranium enlivens feelings of balance, peace, and joyfulness. This scent helps us to relax so we may experience peace and well-being. It supports the nervous system by reducing tension and stress. Geranium's fragrance is uplifting and supportive of romance.

Orange brings peace and harmony to the mind and body. It opens the emotional center of the heart to joy, assisting in overcoming depression.

Myrtle was considered the sacred plant of Aphrodite, the Greek goddess of beauty and love. Its scent is elevating and euphoric. It soothes the emotions and is known to ameliorate feelings of jealousy. It is used in love potions.

Chamomile (Roman, German, and blue) is very effective for relieving stress and nervousness, panic and anxiety states, tension, and grief. Chamomile helps release anger and creates calm within the mind, body, and emotions.

Ginger raises the body temperature and is viewed as an aphrodisiac because of its energizing properties. In South Asia it is added to creams for brides to assist in romance. Ginger helps in combating loneliness and depression.

Sandalwood is useful against tension and anxiety, and is respected as an aphrodisiac for its power to awaken desire.

Cinnamon, a stimulant, is warming to the body and has aphrodisiac properties that may contribute to sexual arousal.

Vanilla is made from the seedpods of orchids and has a warming, cheering scent that helps you get rid of depression, sorrow, and grief. Vanilla elevates the emotions and also is used as an aphrodisiac.

Carnation absolute is a powerful aphrodisiac that also relieves stress-related disorders, especially anxiety. It is spiritually and emotionally uplifting, and expensive.

Black pepper oil, another aphrodisiac, increases self-confidence. It is grounding and stabilizing, and it improves self-image. Black pepper oil is said to heighten alertness and aid in assertiveness. Its stimulating quality makes it useful for emotional and/or mental fatigue.

VASTU TIPS FOR THE BEDROOM

The Vedas extol the virtues of sleep. In fact, they refer to good sleep as a divine gift. Research today shows more and more that lack of sleep contributes to physical and mental disorders. Suffice it to say that to attract and nourish a healthy, fulfilling relationship, good sleep is a must. Vastu offers many practical solutions to eliminate stress in the bedroom and improve the quality of sleep. Below are some easy-to-implement tips for creating a peaceful and harmonious bedroom.

REMINDERS

Sharp or piercing corners create an uneasy, stressful feeling, especially in the bedroom. Eliminate their effect by a hanging a clear crystal, or even wind chimes, in front of the sharp corner.

Hang a twenty-millimeter blue crystal in the northwest corner of your bedroom to stimulate clarity, improve relationships, and create harmony.

ADDITIONAL SUGGESTIONS

❊ If you have a mirror facing the bed, it is best to remove the mirror. When you sleep, stress and tired energy leave your body. If there is a mirror facing the bed, it will reflect the stress and tiredness back to you. Remove mirrors that are opposite the bed for better sleep.

❊ If you have a television in the bedroom, cover it with silk at night. Even when it's turned off, a television leaks radiation, adding stress to the environment.

❊ Turn off your phone at night. Having a phone in the bedroom can interfere with restful sleep.

❊ A large, square-shaped rock placed directly under the head of your bed will ground the energy for a more restful night's sleep. It is recommended not to use granite.

❊ To attract a loving relationship and to improve sleep, place a Moon Yantra in the very center of your bed underneath the mattress, either between it and the box spring or on the floor. Go to *http:// www.makingroomformrright.com* and download a

Moon Yantra, print it, cut the square design out of the paper, lift your mattress, and place it in the exact center.

Be open to exploring new things. Too often we forget the joy and excitement that is ours when we open to new experiences. Will you move through your days with a sense of adventure, or feeling bored, listless, and uninspired? Trying new things can be infinitely rewarding. You may find yourself happily surprised with your discoveries.

Make time to take care of yourself. It is just as important to rest and relax each day as it is to be active. Without downtime, stress builds and eventually takes a toll on your physical and mental health. Taking action to create a restful environment and cultivate restful sleep has enormous benefits.

See your uniqueness and value it. You are unique and perfect just as you are. Your essence, the temple of your being, is like no other and is full of beauty. Just as no two snowflakes are alike, there is no one just like you in this entire world. The divine spark of perfection dwells within you. Experimenting with and using all or some of the techniques in this chapter will help you feel your magnificence and support you to believe in all that you are.

Lori, Faith, and Sasha along with Corrine, Charlene, and Mary—one of Faith's friends from church—are meeting to discuss the use of essential oils, stones, gems, crystals, colors, and Vastu tips. Let's check in on their process of discovery.

Sharing Vedic Tools and Tips

The friends had decided to go to the crystal and rock shop in town, and then head into the city and go to one of the small shops known for its high-quality essential oils. Lori and Sasha swung by Faith's to pick her up for their outing—they were meeting the other women at the rock shop—and found that a physical transformation had happened in Faith. She'd had her hair cut and colored.

Along with her new exercise regime, Faith had known it was time to do more to her hair than use a rubber band to keep it out of her face. Sitting in the beauty salon chair and looking at herself, she saw she had let herself go. She hadn't thought about her appearance in a long time; it was time to try something new. She looked terrific. Sasha and Lori were impressed.

When they got to the shop, Mary noticed Faith's hair immediately and high-fived her, complimenting her on how good she looked. Mary, Faith's friend from church, was around Faith's age and had been coloring her hair and taking care of her appearance in general since her twenties. Not only that, she went to the gym regularly, ate carefully, and although in her mid-fifties, looked forty. A lot of that was her attitude: she refused to buy into any stereotypes about age or beauty. Mary's openness was why Faith knew she would embrace Vastu.

Charlene and Corrine complimented Faith until finally Faith raised her hands in exasperation. She realized that she was going to have to get used to all these compliments about her physical appearance. "Okay, I believe you all. Thank you! Let's go into the shop, shall we?"

The women were enthralled with the array of crystals. Sasha was interested in the energetic and physical properties of the gems and stones, and found someone to answer her questions. When they left, Lori, Faith, and Sasha each had a small bag of loose stones for their altars and some extra pieces they were drawn to that would be placed on desks and bedside tables. Faith purchased a large piece of amethyst for her mantel and to use on the Full Moon Altar as the earth element the following month.

Corrine, Charlene, and Mary also bought some stones for their altars—they were definitely into Vastu. Next, the group drove into Seattle to a store where the shopkeeper gave them an excellent overview of scents and could answer all their questions. Each purchased a small amount of several of the scents they tested and were drawn to, knowing they would experiment with mixing them to find their own personalized scent.

At lunch the women talked about Vastu generally and then about tips for boosting the "romance factor," as Faith called it. The newcomers listened carefully as Faith, Sasha, and Lori shared.

FAITH

One tip Faith had followed was to hang a piece of silk fabric over the television in her bedroom. Lori had mentioned that televisions leak radiation at night, which can interfere with sleep. She also unplugged her TV at night. Just the thought of radiation in the room while she slept totally turned her off.

SASHA

Sasha also covered her TV, but since watching it in bed at night was one of her favorite pastimes, she didn't unplug it. She did, however, turn it off before she fell asleep. Sasha also remembered that she owned a set of pink sheets, and she put them on her bed. She loved sleeping on them and planned to buy another set so she could rotate them.

LORI

Lori had put a square rock just at the top of her bed, on the floor directly under where her head rested at night. She was sleeping better because of it. She also had moved the mirror from over her dresser, which was exactly opposite her bed. She said that the move changed how the room felt. As a gift for both Faith and Sasha, Lori also had ordered blue crystals to hang over their Relationship Altars.

THEIR FRIENDS

Charlene shared that she had already set up her Relationship Altar after decluttering with the help of her husband and boys. "My husband seems very intrigued by the altar," she said smiling. "He kids me about it, but he's also asking a lot of questions. That's a good sign as far as I'm concerned."

Corrine, Sasha's assistant, also shared that she had created a Relationship Altar after doing the Process of Attraction. "That was eye-opening," she admitted, shaking her head. "Now, when I meditate before the altar, I hold the thought of the qualities I want in a man in my mind and just sort of let it sit there as I focus on my breath. It feels good." Sasha didn't mention that she had noticed that Corrine and Jeff, one of the other IT members, had been spending a lot of time together.

Mary shared with the women that she and Alice, another friend of Faith's from church, had started decluttering. Mary asked a lot of questions about the Relationship Altar, and Faith suggested that she do the Process of Attraction first. Mary agreed.

"On the next full moon, I think it would be great to do another Full Moon Altar," Lori said, smiling expansively. "Why don't you all come, and invite anybody else you know who would be interested?"

"That's a great idea," Sasha agreed. "I want to invite Elliott, too."

They talked about expanding the circle. Lori thought it would be wonderful to invite her yoga class. The enthusiasm was palpable at the table. "I can't think of a more wonderful way to expand the power of love and Vastu than to come together on the full moon," Faith said, smiling from ear to ear. "We could talk about the other things we've done to create balance and harmony in our homes, if other people want to know. We could make it a regular monthly event." She was suddenly excited by this idea.

"We might need to change locations if everyone we're thinking of inviting wanted to come," Lori said, envisioning Faith's home overcrowded with new friends.

Faith quickly began mentally scouting possible venues. The auditorium at her church or Lori's yoga studio instantly came to mind. "I can check with my church, and Lori, would you check with your yoga studio? Those are two possibilities right off the bat . . ."

Looking forward to their future together with anticipation, the women parted feeling bolstered by the conversation and new possibilities. Sasha drove Faith and Lori home, and broached her concern about feeling so vulnerable. She could barely work and was having crazy thoughts about Elliott all the time, intimate and otherwise. She didn't want to blow it by being too needy or possessive. She had discovered a well of insatiable desire for a guy who a few weeks before didn't seem interested in her at all and vice versa. She now wanted everything with him. She was concerned she was going crazy.

"No crazier than anyone else in the world who's falling in love," Faith commented drily. "You're feeling what it's like for you to fall in love with a man. It's what you wanted. It's just new terrain. There's no 'right' way to do it. We all do it in our own way. I think you're more prepared than ever, and I don't think you would even have noticed him if you hadn't opened up your heart some and decided it was time to feel this depth of emotion. I'm happy for you." Faith smiled. "I think you should celebrate."

"I do, too," Lori added, knowing what a big change it was for Sasha to talk about her deepest feelings with such openness. "I don't think you're reacting unusually. When love is met with love, it only grows. I think we all need to be reminded of this. When it's right, it's right."

Sasha dropped Faith and Lori at Faith's house. She was meeting Elliott at his store and going to a movie and dinner. Happy and busy, she thought. Imagine that.

LORI

Faith asked Lori in for a cup of tea, and as Faith turned the heat on under the kettle, she looked out the window and saw the contractor next door. "Remember the interesting guy I met who's doing the remodel next door? I'd like to introduce you to him. He's such a nice guy. I see he's there now. Let's go over and say hi. All right?"

"Sure," Lori said, moving quickly as Faith made a bee-line through the kitchen doorway. "I'd love to meet him. Hey, wait up!"

Faith cut through a path in the side hedge that bordered the two houses as Lori followed closely behind. The contractor turned to see them coming toward him. Faith called out. "Hi, Ben! How are you doing today? I wanted to introduce you to my friend."

"Lori?" Ben said, surprised and delighted to see this particular pretty face.

"Ben?" Lori said, eyes wide and shocked to see this grown man who was her close friend growing up. "Oh my God! How are you? How long has it been? It has to be at least twenty-five years. You don't look any different." She stopped herself, realizing she wasn't giving Ben any time to respond. She rushed forward and gave him a hug.

"Well, it's obvious you two know each other," Faith said, intrigued by the electrical energy between the two.

"What a surprise—Lori! Yes, Faith," Ben replied, looking toward Faith. "Lori was my best friend growing up. I can't believe you're here." Holding Lori's hands, he looked into her eyes. "You haven't changed a bit, just gotten prettier. How's Rick? You must have kids, too," he added.

Lori told Ben about her divorce and her daughters. Rick had remarried, had his own life. Saying this made Lori realize that it didn't sadden her any longer to think about her ex or what he was doing with his life. These were huge strides in the right direction, she acknowledged silently to herself.

Ben hadn't come back after attending college in Southern California, and his family had moved south to be near him. He had married while in school and had four children, one right after the other. They were all grown now, and he even had a grandchild. His wife and he had divorced about ten years before, and she had remarried. He had been in the IT industry and worked his way up to an executive position, where he stayed until he realized enough was enough. It wasn't his passion; building was. He had been doing remodels and new construction, more for the fun of it, for the past five years. He had been back in the Seattle area for about a year and a half.

They continued to catch up, Lori reminding him of the fort Ben and his dad had built in the backyard when they were probably in third grade, when Faith interrupted.

"I need to go back to the house and turn off the heat on the stove. Why don't you come over in a few minutes for tea, Ben? Bring Lori with you." Faith gave Lori a wink and

turned to walk back to her house as Lori and Ben continued talking.

"I thought about you a lot," Ben said, "but I didn't try
to contact you because I knew how jealous Rick used to be
when we'd hang out together. I just didn't think that you'd
ever be divorced."

"As you know, these things happen in life. You don't
plan them to happen, they just do." Lori looked wistfully
into his eyes, thinking of lost opportunities.

"It's so good to see you!" Ben said, still in shock that
this beautiful woman who was his best friend growing up,
the girl he quietly loved, stood right in front of him. "I just
can't get over that you're here."

"I know . . . it's pretty amazing, but then there's been
a lot of amazing things happening lately, so in a way I
shouldn't be surprised to see you," Lori said as she realized how serendipitous this was and yet how perfect.
Ben had been her constant friend, the one person she
confided in. When she and Rick began dating in high
school, he had made it clear to her that he didn't want
to share his girl with another guy, even Ben. Being
young and in love, she did whatever Rick asked, even
letting go of the one relationship that meant the most
to her.

"Let's go over to Faith's for tea," Ben said. "We've got

all the time in the world to catch up." He put his arm around Lori's shoulder, like old times.

"Yes, we do." Lori turned her head and looked into his eyes as she put her arm around his waist. Such a familiar gesture, she realized. So familiar . . . and so right.

Sometimes the heart sees what

is invisible to the eye.

—H. JACKSON BROWN JR.

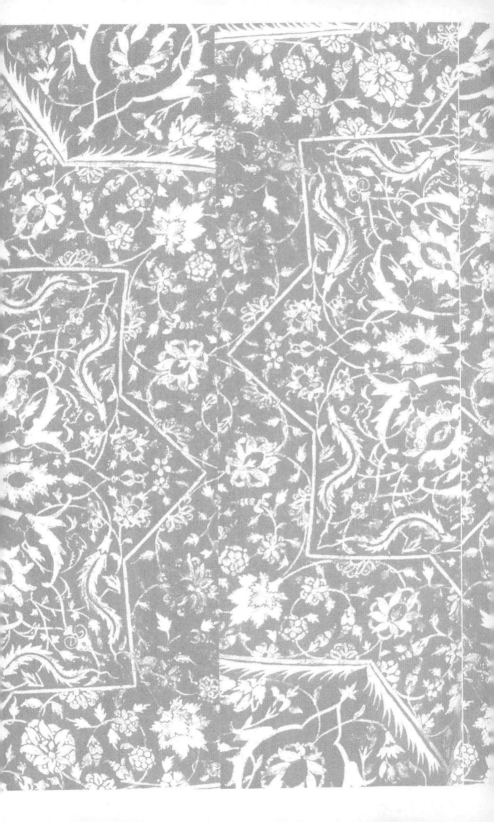

CHAPTER NINE

Treating Yourself Right: Bringing Balance to Mind, Body, and Spirit

n o matter how much love other people have for us, or how much they express it, unless we love ourselves, we can't feel it deeply and respond. Vastu addresses healthy self-love in a brilliant way: it's all about balance. According to Vastu, bringing balance into our lives through loving acts cultivates the vibrant energy of attraction. The six time-tested Vedic techniques in this chapter contribute to good health and support balance and harmony within the mind/body/spirit.

Action Step 7
Bringing Your Awareness
to Loving Acts

These purifying techniques are based on Ayurveda, the world's oldest medical system, which originated in Vedic times. Their use will eliminate varying degrees of stress or disease, invigorate your physiology, positively influence your health, and, when practiced regularly, help you feel younger, happier, and healthier. It almost goes without saying that all of this makes you more attractive and desirable.

THE ADDED BENEFITS

Just as with daily practice at your altar, doing these techniques regularly and lovingly sends a message to the divine that you know you matter and are worthy of love. The universe already knows this, and when you know it, too, you are connected: grace flows, joy grows, and opportunities appear. In committing to loving acts, you put the universe on notice that you are ready to step into the flow of giving and receiving. From this place of expanded possibility, your heart fills with the gratitude and grace that you have always desired. From here, transformation occurs.

These practices are in a specific order to do first thing in the morning, but you can pick and choose which ones to implement. Start with two, adding others as you become comfortable and wish to expand your set of morning rituals.

As with any health program, we recommend that you check with your health practitioner before performing any of the exercises here.

START AT THE TOP: PURIFYING THE TONGUE

When most people wake in the morning, their tongue feels fuzzy. It's because while we sleep, toxins gather in the mouth due to incomplete or improper digestion. Tongue scraping removes the yellowish coating—called *ama* in Sanskrit—that builds up overnight and needs to be eliminated first thing in the morning. Otherwise the body reabsorbs it.

Western medicine and modern research have concluded that removing this layer of plaque and bacteria reduces the risk of bad breath, gum disease, throat infections, tooth decay, and even heart disease. Tongue scrapers can be purchased at grocery and health food stores and online. They come in a variety of metals, as well as plastic, and are indispensable for your good health.

Follow these simple steps

As soon as you get out of bed in the morning, before you drink any water or eat any food, do this technique.

- Gently hold the tongue scraper and scrape it from the back of your tongue to the tip. Use a light pressure to avoid gagging and any discomfort.

- Scrape the tongue three to five times until the coating on your tongue is removed.

- Rinse the tongue scraper before repeating.

- When finished, rinse out your mouth, then rinse and dry the tongue scraper.

- As with a toothbrush, do not share your scraper.

DETOXIFYING THE BODY—ABHYANGA (AH-BEE-YAN-GA)

Every day our bodies are exposed to toxins; removing them daily makes sense. Abhyanga is a kind of self-massage using an oil bath and gentle stroking to remove toxins and stimulate the movement of energy in the body. Best done in the morning before showering, abhyanga improves blood and lymph circulation, eliminates muscle tension and fatigue, and has a tonifying influence on the immune system.

A complete session takes about five or ten minutes. Use organic cold-pressed sesame oil, which you can purchase in glass bottles at grocery or health food stores. Sesame oil has many healing properties, as it is an antioxidant as well as a wonderful moisturizer for the skin. If you are sensitive to it, try another moisturizing and conditioning oil, such as olive, coconut, or almond.

To prepare for your abhyanga massage, heat the oil by putting the bottle in a sink filled with warm water for a few minutes. The warmed oil is soothing when applied and readily absorbed into the skin. You can either apply the oil standing in the shower or standing or sitting on a towel on the bathroom floor. You don't need a lot of oil, only an ounce or two for the whole body—just enough to cover the skin with a thin coating.

As you apply the oil, pay attention to your breath and keep your awareness on what you are doing. Consider this a healing ritual that supports your health and well-being. The more you can attend to this process with awareness, the more beneficial the experience will be for you.

HEAD AND NECK MASSAGE

If you wash your hair every day, you can do this head and neck massage daily. If you don't wash your hair daily, use it whenever you do. Before you wash your hair, put a little oil (sesame, olive, or coconut) on your hands and apply the oil to your scalp, using the palm of your hand, in a circular motion. With your fingertips, rub oil behind your ears and earlobes, pulling your earlobes down lightly at the end of each stroke. This feels great and also stimulates tiny energetic healing points on the ears. Next, stroke your forehead in a back-and-forth motion with the palm of your hand. Then massage the rest of the face, paying attention to your jaw joints and temples. Use an upward motion to massage the neck in front and a downward motion on the back of the neck. Now you are ready for the rest of the massage.

THE BODY MASSAGE

The body massage can be done vigorously and quickly. The resulting feeling of well-being lasts all day.

Here are two methods. The first is good for waking up the body, and the second has a more purifying affect on the energetic field. Try both and see which one feels more appropriate for you on any given day. Be sure to focus on what you are doing. Bring your awareness to feeling the oil being applied to your body. Your focused attention will enhance the healing quality of the massage.

For both methods, use the palm of your hand in a circular motion around the joints (elbows, knees, wrists, and ankles). On the bones of your arms and legs, use longer strokes.

Mary Jo Cravatta's Abhyanga

❀ Begin with three circular strokes on your shoulder, then stroke up and down five times on your upper arm, being sure to get the outside and inside of your arm.

❀ Next, do a circular motion three times on your elbow and up and down five times on your lower arm.

❀ Use a circular motion on your wrist and up and down on your metacarpal bones (bones of the fingers).

❀ Massage your chest five times in a back-and-forth motion with the palm of your hand.

❀ Massage around your breasts with a circular motion toward the breastbone five times with the palm of your hand. Then reverse the circle in the opposite direction, again five times.

❀ Next, massage your abdominal area clockwise (in the direction of your colon: up the right side, then across the stomach, and down the left side) three to five times.

❀ Work your way down your body: thighs, buttocks, knees, shins, calves, ankles, feet (tops and bottoms), and toes.

Vaidya Mishra's Abhyanga

❀ On all joints, do three circular strokes.

❀ Do seven long strokes down from the shoulder and out the fingertips on the front of the arm; repeat on the back of the arm.

❀ Do seven strokes down the chest with both hands.

❀ Do seven clockwise circles around the abdomen.

❀ If you are agile and can manage, or have help, do seven long strokes down your back and buttocks.

❀ Do three circular strokes on the hips.

❀ Go down the legs and out the toes, front and back, again seven times. Don't forget to do three circular strokes around both of your knees and elbows, wrists, and ankles.

Other Points to Keep in Mind

❀ When showering, use as little soap as possible, and only when and where really needed. Soap tends to dry the skin.

❀ Use a pine cleanser to remove oil residue from your shower/bathtub and towels after oil massage. Use a detergent booster such as Arm & Hammer Washing Soda weekly to clear drains.

OIL PULLING

Written about in an Ayurvedic text called the *Charaka Samhita*, this technique is helpful in healing many conditions, including asthma, headaches, aches and pains, and diabetes. It's been said to whiten teeth and make your skin look radiant.

Oil pulling needs to be done on an empty stomach in the morning.

❀ Take one tablespoon of sesame oil or sunflower oil in the mouth and swish it around for approximately fifteen to twenty minutes, or until the oil is white. If it is yellow, the process is not complete.

❀ Do not gargle with the oil and do not swallow it.

❀ When you spit it out, rinse your mouth with water thoroughly. Rinsing is essential so you don't inadvertently swallow any of the oil.

The Power of Yoga

After your shower, and before you do any other spiritual practices such as Vedic breathing, chanting, or meditation, do some simple yoga postures for strength and flexibility. Yoga brings substantial benefits to the mind, body, and spirit. There are many books, videos, DVDs, and classes dedicated to the practice of yoga, and we encourage you to explore this magnificent tool and begin a practice of your own.

Yoga lubricates the joints, tendons, and ligaments of the body; tones the inner organs; and creates feelings of strength, confidence, and lightness. It can be done at any age, so you're never too young or too old to begin. Even beginners enjoy the benefits of yoga simply by doing a series of exercises that move the spine in six directions—side to side, front to back, and twisting the torso from left to right in rhythm with the breath. These simple movements stimulate the energy that runs up and down the spine, and circulates that energy throughout the organs of the body.

Below is a simple exercise for relieving neck and shoulder tension that you can do in a chair at work, at home, even on an airplane. You can try it right now.

YOGA FOR THE NECK AND SHOULDERS

❂ Sit with your spine erect and shoulders relaxed.

❂ Take a deep breath in through the nose, and as you breathe out (through the mouth), drop your chin to your chest.

❂ Continue with long, slow, deep breaths in and out through the nose as you begin to rotate your head to the right very slowly.

❂ As you move your head, feel the contraction on one side of your neck and the stretch on the other.

❀ When you come across an area that feels stiff, pause and breathe into the sensation in long, slow, deep breaths, in and out through the nose. Imagine the tension melting like warm butter.

❀ Continue your neck rotation, moving your head to the right shoulder, then to the back, and finally to the left shoulder, very easily, in a slowly moving circle.

❀ When you get to the front, with your chin dropped to your chest, reverse the direction and rotate slowly from left to right.

❀ Once you have completed a full rotation in each direction, bring your head up to center and take a deep breath in through the nose, exhaling through the mouth, and relax. Close your eyes and feel the energy moving in the area of the neck.

Living in the Present Moment

Have you ever observed your mind? You have probably noticed that it moves from one thought to the next, from the past to the future, to some regret or disappointment, or something you are anticipating. Rarely if ever do we actually feel what is occurring in the present moment.

Sri Sri Ravi Shankar, a renowned spiritual leader of India, once said that the present moment is inevitable. It is the only place where you can experience what joy truly is. He also said that love is more than an emotion; it is your very nature: you are love. Yet this love, this experience of love of self, rarely is felt because the mind vacillates from the past to the future, keeping us occupied and distracted from our essential self, which is filled with love *now*. Only within this present moment, this now, do we exist in all our power, all our true potential.

It makes sense, then, to live in the present moment. But, you may ask, how? The answer is so simple, it is hard to believe: through the breath. Our breath is the link between the mind, the emotions, and the body. By focusing on our breathing, we can experience this moment right now.

Specific breathing exercises, called *pranayama* (pra-na-ya-ma), release stress and change the quality of our thoughts, feelings, and perceptions so we can be fully in the moment, comfortably. When the mind relaxes, the natural joy within us can arise. When it does, we realize that everything is really fine in this moment, right now.

ALTERNATE NOSTRIL BREATHING

To give you an experience of how the breath can influence your mind, here's a wonderful pranayama called, in Sanskrit, *nadi shodhana*, or alternate nostril breathing. This exercise balances the left and the right hemispheres of the brain and reduces mental chatter.

❋ Sit with your eyes closed, spine erect, and shoulders relaxed.

❋ Breathe from the diaphragm in a relaxed fashion, keeping the inhalation and exhalation slow and even throughout this breathing exercise.

❋ Use the thumb and the forefinger of the right hand to alternately close each nostril during the exercise.

❋ Begin by closing the right nostril with your right thumb, and slowly exhaling and inhaling through the left nostril.

❋ Now close off the left nostril with your right forefinger, and slowly exhale and inhale through the right nostril.

❀ Complete the exercise by doing nine repetitions of breathing through the left and the right nostrils in this fashion.

❀ When complete, relax your hands, placing them face up on your knees.

❀ Take a moment and feel the *prana*, or life force energy, moving through your body.

Slowly, gradually, in your own time, open your eyes.

Sudarshan Kriya

This breathing process is a purifying exercise. *Su* means proper or true in Sanskrit; *darshan* means vision. *Kriya* refers to a purifying action using the breath. Sudarshan kriya gives you a true vision of who you really are, without fear and without resistance—which could be considered emotional impurities. Through this simple technique you can experience your true self, which is a very natural, very easy feeling. This exercise is energizing and rejuvenating and is used daily by people around the world because of its many benefits.

For more information and to learn this powerful technique, visit the Web site provided in the resources section at the back of this book.

Putting It All Together: Meditation

After your morning practices is the perfect time to meditate. If you already have a practice, you know that meditation clears the mind and reduces stress. By taking twenty minutes to refresh your nervous system and connect with deeper levels of your consciousness, you can enter your day with added awareness and creativity.

If you don't meditate now, please consider beginning. There are many ways to learn—from books and CDs to organizations that teach specific practices. (Please see the resources section at the back of this book.) Over the years more and more people have realized the benefits of meditation. Reputable institutions, including the University of California at Los Angeles, Harvard University, Stanford University, and the National Institutes of Health have conducted hundreds of studies on its effects. It has been shown not only to reduce the risk of stroke and heart attack but also to reduce high blood pressure and cholesterol, support immune system response, and improve sleep.

Research has shown that we use only about 10 percent of our mental capacity. Through meditation we can access more of our brain's potential. In a nutshell, meditation enhances your health and helps you think and act more clearly. It positively affects every area of life, including your relationships.

Here is a meditation you can do right now to experience the positive effect it can have on your life. If you would like to listen to a guided version of this meditation, go to the Web site at *http://www.makingroomformr right.com*.

THE FIVE-ELEMENT RELATIONSHIP MEDITATION

❀ Find a place where you will not be disturbed.

❀ Sit comfortably with your eyes closed.

❀ Take a deep breath in and let go.

❀ Become aware of the earth element within the body. Your flesh and bones are part of the earth element. By becoming aware of the earth element in the body, you can bring it into balance.

❀ Experience the feeling of being supported in all your present and future relationships.

✿ You are now in balance with the earth element.

✿ Take a deep breath in and let go.

✿ Become aware of the water element within the body. Your bodily fluids are part of the water element. By becoming aware of the water element in the body, you can bring it into balance.

✿ Experience the feeling of growth in all your relationships.

✿ You are now in balance with the water element.

✿ Take a deep breath in and let go.

✿ Become aware of the fire element within the body. Your bodily warmth is part of the fire element. By becoming aware of the fire element in the body, you can bring it into balance.

✿ Experience the feeling of passion in your relationships.

✿ You are now in balance with the fire element.

✿ Take a deep breath in and let go.

✿ Become aware of the air element within the body. Your breath is part of the air element. By becoming aware of the air element in the body, you can bring it into balance.

❀ Experience the feeling of harmonious communication in your relationships.

❀ You are now in balance with the air element.

❀ Take a deep breath in and let go.

❀ Become aware of the space element within the body. The space within your body is part of the space element. By becoming aware of the space element in the body, you can bring it into balance.

❀ Experience the feeling of being successful in your relationships.

❀ You are now in balance with the space element.

❀ Take a deep breath in and let go.

❀ You are a part of the same five elements that exist in nature. Experience the feeling of being in harmony with nature within and around you, and bless all your relationships, past, present, and future.

❀ Chant *Om Shanti, Shanti, Shanti.* (May there be peace and harmony in all your relationships.)

As you begin to incorporate these practices into your life, we guarantee that you will find positive changes in the way you feel. All change begins within. We hope that you will establish a daily practice of these techniques and share them with others.

A Pledge to Yourself

We invite you to make a vow now that for the next forty consecutive days you will integrate these practices into your daily routine. Be aware of any changes you notice. You might want to purchase a journal or a notebook to record your experiences. Every day, thank yourself for these loving gifts. You are in the midst of a life-changing experience, a rejuvenation of self, a rebirth even, that can continue for the rest of your life.

Now is the time. So often, our responsibilities to others, or what appear to be priorities, pull us away from taking the time to give to ourselves first. Choose to make loving changes in your life, now. You are worth it!

Peace and fulfillment are possible. Put your attention on what you want. Choose to focus your thoughts on peace and fulfillment.

Commitment yields great rewards. Commit to loving your-self the way you wish to be loved. What goes around, comes around.

Sasha, Lori, and Faith Add Morning Rituals

For as long as she could remember, Lori woke up early in the morning for what she called her "quiet time." As a young girl she would start her day with her diary and reading something that she enjoyed. Since learning about yoga and Vastu, she had begun to explore other practices from Eastern traditions. She read voraciously about techniques and ancient systems, then applied the ones that intrigued her. She shared all of these with Sasha and Faith.

You might feel drawn to some of these methods and not others like Faith and Sasha, who were resistant to the oil pulling technique. It wasn't until Lori told them that people had started asking her why her skin was glowing that both Sasha and Faith became willing to try it. And when she told them that her dentist said her gums were in better shape than they'd been in years and that her teeth were whiter, Faith and Sasha were definitely in.

Lori also talked to Sasha about doing yoga with Elliott,

and Faith decided that she'd ask Chris if he'd like to take one of the classes that Lori taught on the weekends. "Great," Lori said, envisioning new possibilities. "Why don't you do a presentation about the Full Moon Ceremony when you come?"

"Well . . . okay," Faith replied, willing to take on any challenge these days. "That will be fun, I guess. It might get people interested in the next gathering."

The women had already decided to do the next Full Moon Ceremony at the studio; Lori had booked it for the next six months.

"Are you going to invite Ben?" Sasha asked her.

"Probably," replied Lori, remembering a conversation she and Ben had had recently. "I found out he's taken a Vedic breathing class, so I'm sure he'll be open to this. At least I think so."

"I felt there was something different about him," Faith, an astute observer of people, thoughtfully replied. "He seems so relaxed and comfortable with himself, and he's so down-to-earth in a very nice way."

"Well, he's always been a great guy, but I noticed that about him, too. This practice gets rid of so much stress and tension, and when it's gone, you feel like you're connected to everyone in some way. It's great."

Finally, Lori encouraged Faith and Sasha to learn the art

of meditation. Lori called it an art because learning to just "be," to do absolutely nothing, and to find that space where time does not exist creates a kind of beauty that can only be experienced. It's not dreaming, it's not thinking; it's diving into the silence between each thought, and experiencing nothing and everything all at the same time.

"I don't know if I can describe it in words," Lori said, pausing before she attempted to explain. "I've had this experience in meditation where my mind has quieted down and released its hold on my spirit, and it felt so good! I entered a realm where all discomfort dissolved. I felt expanded and exhilarated. It was blissful—you are totally and undeniably in the present moment. Of course as soon as you realize that you are there, you come out of it.

"But the point is, if you meditate regularly, you'll notice that you're kinder to yourself in your daily life—it's just a by-product of it. That's the real test: when your outer world becomes the expression of a full, loving heart, you know your practice is true. In loving yourself, you are not taking it from a limited resource; and when you give, you are not giving your life force. You have more than enough to share because you are receiving from the source of consciousness that flows within you."

Faith and Sasha knew that Lori had found an inner peace and calmness and they wanted it for themselves, so they committed to taking a meditation class; not just for themselves, either, but because they thought they could benefit others by being kinder and calmer. Ultimately, they had learned that by aligning with their inner self, their spirit, they would be in the right place to experience all the love they could hold.

As they would share the benefits of their practices and the results of their work with their friends, they knew their already expanding little circle would continue to grow. Each was more aware than ever of the fertile possibilities growing in their lives. So much of what had changed had been fed by their willingness to remain open, curious, and trusting in what cannot be seen, only felt with the heart. This awareness gave them more than enough faith that the future would unfold with continued blessings.

> You learn to speak by speaking, to study by studying, to run by running, to work by working; and just so, you learn to love by loving.
>
> —ST. FRANCIS DE SALES

CHAPTER TEN

Fine-Tuning Your Environment: A Green Living Solution

If you have followed the steps of *Making Room for Mr. Right*, no doubt you are feeling the positive effects of Vastu. But if you still have low energy, insomnia, or feel tired even if you get enough sleep, you may be suffering from a kind of stress that isn't triggered by the usual culprits—traffic, crowds, noise, financial concerns, over-committed or undercommitted social life, not enough exercise, too much sugar or caffeine, relationship issues, and so on.

There's another kind of stress triggered by energy that emanates from natural phenomena such as underground streams, fault lines, and radiation, as well as man-made energy conductors such as tunnels and lines that carry water, sewage, and electricity.

This energy, or geopathic stress, may cause symptoms such as headaches, muscle aches and cramps, nightmares, even teeth grinding, and it exacerbates the other stresses you feel. Some studies suggest that geopathic stress leads to more serious conditions. Many European countries take geopathic stress seriously enough that builders are required to have their properties surveyed for geopathic stress before they build on them.

There is no need for you to become an expert on geopathic stress, but it is helpful to have a basic understanding of it. When you go about eliminating it, which we will share with you, you will experience the existence of this invisible force and how to block its effects. The technique is simple and fun to do.

Geopathic stress impacts us most wherever we spend a great deal of time. For most of us that's where we sleep and where we sit at work. The key to understanding this kind of stress and its undesirability is that wherever two or more geopathic stress lines cross, radiation builds and over time can inhibit the immune system, which can lead to disease.

Stress, coming from earth imbalances such as natural streams running under your home, tunnels, electrical lines, sewage lines, storm drains, and more, affects our bodies, minds, and inevitably our emotions. Wherever geopathic stress is found, the element associated with that direction also is influenced.

For example, when *water* beneath your home or office runs from *northwest* to *southeast*, you will feel depleted and, logically, you lack enthusiasm or passion in general. The Vastu reason is that water's influence in the southeast reduces or dilutes the heat of the *fire* element— that's the fire needed to create passion.

Streams and water flowing through pipes under your home or office and coming in or out through the *south*, *southwest*, or *west* undermine stability and support from friends, family, and coworkers. The water's movement in these directions disrupts the *earth* element, which is associated with support.

Underground water that runs beneath the *center* of your home, which is the area of the *space element*, affects success in future relationships.

In the case of electrical wiring and cables, which are associated with the *fire* element, when they enter a house from the *north, northeast, or east* (areas associated with the water element) they inhibit relationship growth.

Fault lines (related to the *air* element) running under the *northwest* area of your home have a negative influence on the mind, especially your ability to communicate, which can be a problem in relationships.

Geopathic Stress and the Eight Directions

Geopathic stress influences our lives depending on which direction it is in or comes from.

Stress in the northwest area of your home affects your emotions and communication with others. In the north this stress can make you feel ungrateful and needy. Stress in the northeast can block you spiritually and prevent you from experiencing synchronicity. Stress coming from the east influences health; in the southeast your natural magnetism lacks vibrancy; in the south it affects self-esteem. In the southwest, geopathic stress blocks supportive friendships and connections with others. This stress located in the west blocks creativity and causes mental and sometimes physical rigidity.

Again, if you feel blocked or lack energy in any area of your life, you probably will find it difficult to attract or enjoy a positive relationship. Eliminating environmental obstructions releases the energy necessary to move forward and feel happy. Don't overlook this important area of stress reduction. In stress-free, healthy environments, energy flows freely: you feel connected to nature and your own natural rhythms. You receive more of what you want in life, including a wonderful man to share it with.

Have we convinced you how important it is to find and eliminate any geopathic stress affecting you? The good news is that you can clear its effects easily. Here's how.

Action Step 8
Clearing Environmental Stress

This simple technique has been used by thousands of our clients over the years. One of the best times to do it is on a full moon day when we humans are most sensitive to environmental energy. We suggest doing it within the twenty-four-hour period leading up to the full moon, not after it. The moon's energy at this time is most conducive for this kind of work. But any time is a good time to remove environmental stress, so don't wait: Just do it!

HOW TO PREPARE

You will need a few items to begin.

1. Two dowsing rods. You can use two wire coat hangers for each rod or purchase copper wiring (see below).

2. Ten to twelve straight pieces of #4 copper wire, either nine inches or eighteen inches long, to be used as copper staples. You can purchase the wire online or at a local hardware store. You can ask the store to cut the wire for you, or purchase wire cutters and do it yourself.

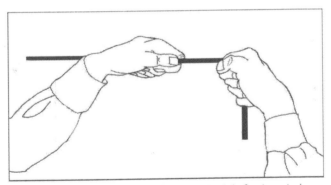

Dowsing rod: Each rod should be approximately fourteen inches long. Make a four-inch bend on one end so the rod becomes L-shaped with a four-inch handle. The size of these rods can vary. The idea is to have about a four-inch handle and an extension of at least ten inches or more in length. You also can use a wire coat hanger to make the dowsing rod.

3. A compass for determining the directions. This can be purchased in a sporting goods store where there are hiking or camping supplies, or online. An inexpensive one will work fine.

ON THE DAY OF THE FULL MOON

In the morning, upon arising bathe and put on clean clothes. As with any of the action steps, intention is the key to success.

After bathing, if you meditate or have a breathing, chanting, or yoga practice, make time for yourself to do at least twenty minutes of your practice. Taking time for yourself in this way has a wonderful effect on you and your outlook. It also relaxes and opens you to the energy used for dowsing.

THE PROCESS

To begin, hold the short end of the L-shaped coat hanger or dowsing rod in each hand, keeping your grip light so the rods are able to move easily.

Whether you are doing the outside or the inside of your home or office, always do this process in a clockwise motion, starting in the northwest.

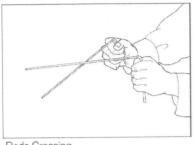
Rods Crossing

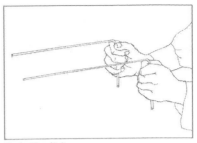
Rods Parallel

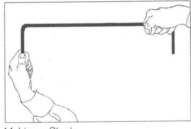
Making a Staple

Close your eyes and take some long, deep, slow breaths in and out several times, breathing in through the nose and out through the mouth.

Open your eyes and ask out loud or inside your mind, "Show me the geopathic stress lines that are blocking my health, happiness, and well-being, coming from my left."

Then begin to walk around the perimeter of the house or inside a room in a clockwise manner, holding the rods parallel to each other and parallel to the ground. Where the rods cross, you have located a geopathic stress line.

BLOCKING GEOPATHIC STRESS OUTSIDE

If you live in a home that sits on a piece of property or work in a building where you can check for geopathic stress outside the structure, this process will block stress lines from entering the home or office.

MICHAEL'S VASTU TIP: To see a video of how to do this process, go to *www.makingroomformrright.com.*

Whenever you find geopathic stress, the L-rods will cross.

At that point you will make a copper staple by taking one of the straight eighteen-inch copper rods that have been cut for this purpose and bending each end two inches, forming a giant staple.

Push the bent ends all the way into the ground at right angles (ninety degrees) to where the line is found (see illustration) so the staple is flush to the ground.

Outside: Place Staple at Right Angle to Stress Line

The copper creates an energetic barrier that restricts the geopathic stress from entering the structure.

To make sure you have thoroughly blocked a geopathic stress line, take a few steps back from where the staple has been placed and, as before, close your eyes and take a few deep breaths in through the nose and out through the mouth. Again, ask yourself the above question regarding your health, happiness, and well-being, and begin walking forward with the L-rods parallel to the ground. If you have blocked the stress line correctly, the rods will not cross when you walk forward through it.

Continue walking until your L-rods cross again. Block that stress line and check it as you did above.

Move all the way around the structure until you return to your starting point. Congratulate yourself. You have successfully blocked the geopathic stress.

BLOCKING GEOPATHIC STRESS INSIDE

If you live in an apartment, condominium, or flat, rent a room in a home, or live in a dormitory, check for geopathic stress in the room or rooms where you spend the most time. For most people, it is their bedroom or a home office. Even if you have dowsed outside, it is recommended to check inside your home or office for stress lines. The reason for this is that even if environmental stress lines have been blocked on the outside, electrical wiring and pipes within floors and walls can affect you.

Whenever you find geopathic stress, the L-rods will cross and you will have located a geopathic stress line.

Instead of making a copper staple, you will lay a straight copper rod parallel with the wall everyplace you locate a stress line.

You can tuck the copper rod under the floor molding or lay it very close to the wall, out of the way.

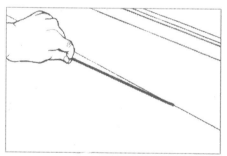

Inside: Block Stress
Line Parallel to Wall

If you find a geopathic stress line in a doorway, it is usually coming from an opposite wall. That is where you will need to place the rod to block the stress.

Make a mental note that if you find two lines crossing in a bedroom or office, to mark where they cross. If they cross on your bed, ask yourself if you have noticed any physical illness, discomfort, or sleep problems. If they cross at your desk or chair at work, ask yourself if you've had trouble concentrating, being productive, or have felt fatigued while at work.

As you eliminate environmental stress and balance the five elements in your living space and work space, you will notice that you feel more peaceful and serene. From a Vastu perspective, your home is the body of your body. Even your office, if you work away from home, influences your overall well-being and joy. By reducing the stress with this technique, energy will flow more freely and you will feel more positive. Creating what you want will be easier.

MICHAEL'S VASTU TIP: From time to time, the earth shifts and you may need to recheck your home and office to make corrections. Do this especially if you notice changes in your sleeping patterns and stress levels.

Do you doubt you're capable of finding geopathic stress? Eighty percent of people can find environmental abnormalities with dowsing. If you doubt your abilities, ask a friend for help and do it together. Once you get the hang of it, it's easy!

Remember, you are in the process of change . . . enjoy it! You have a choice. You can make a difference in your life and embrace the experiences you are having—or not. Try something new and trust in the process!

Anticipate something wonderful! If you locate geopathic stress in your home or work space, you will be surprised at the difference removing it makes in your life. Celebrate the positive changes to come . . . anticipate them!

The Flow of Possibility

On the day of the full moon, Lori, Faith, and Sasha met early in the morning at the hospital where Sasha and Lori worked. Time was limited as the clinic opened early, so the women worked quickly. Each time their dowsing rods crossed, they noticed what might be causing it—electrical outlets and other contributors usually were nearby. Considering how easy the process actually was, once they got the hang of it, they whipped through Lori's office in no time. They also cleared the storage room next door, one that not only needed to be checked for geopathic stress but also cleared of clutter, which contributed to stress.

Sasha and Faith were total believers in the process, now that they had seen the rods crossing as if some invisible hand were drawing them together. They moved eagerly on to Sasha's office in the IT department. The three computers on Sasha's desk and the multitude of wires, plugs, and peripheral electrical items made the room a geopathic land mine. Sasha laid down three copper rods just in the area of her desk. She and Lori did some decluttering and then moved into the outer office area, where there were even more computers, outlets, wiring, and accoutrements of Sasha's IT world. When their work was finished, the office felt completely different—comfortable, clean, and spacious.

While they drove to Faith's, the three friends discussed the relative weirdness of dowsing and its practicality, and decided that weirdness in fact is a matter of perspective. Lori offered her theory of positive change.

"This is how I see it," she began. "You can play it safe for years, never try anything new, convinced that you know how things are supposed to be—you might call it keeping to the straight and narrow. But life gets messy sometimes, and the world can change in a heartbeat—it happened to me, it's happened to all of us. I believe, really and truly, that while change can be scary, it's good! If everything is in your control and under wraps, then nothing new can come to you. Nothing can change.

"We women," she continued thoughtfully, "are programmed not to risk in love or to pursue opportunities. We get scared, or we think it's fear, but really it might just be excitement that we feel, but we mistake it for fear."

"That's right," Faith proclaimed, as she nodded her head in agreement.

"What if all the things we are afraid of are actually things we would find exciting, if we let ourselves?" Lori continued. "I'm not talking about driving too fast or anything harmful, but pushing the boundaries of our little worlds a bit. If we don't, how are we ever going to know if we are living fully?"

After she finished talking, the three were silent the rest of the way to Faith's. Once there, they cleared the outside stress lines, finding several near her bedroom and office. In the process they noticed some scrawny rose bushes right where the geopathic lines ran toward the house. Geopathic stress affects not only humans, but plants and animals as well.

Inside Faith's house they found stress in her office primarily around her computer, printer, fax machine, and scanner, and in her bedroom where two lines converged across her bed. The lines came together right over the middle of her bed, lining up with her stomach when she was sleeping. Faith had experienced indigestion for years. She believed that eliminating the stress line would help her.

They then moved to Sasha's apartment. Sasha dowsed the kitchen first and found a stress line coming in right where a line of ants had been invading her home on and off for years. Lori noted that insects, especially ants, are attracted to geopathic stress.

At Lori's they discovered several lines outside, including one where mold had grown close to the house. Inside, they detected more lines, including one running right across the head of her daughter's bed. Lori remembered that Emma had been complaining of headaches in the morning ever since she moved the bed to that location.

As Sasha, Lori, and Faith finished, they felt they possessed one of the secrets of the universe—and, in a sense, they were right. Sages of long ago told us how to deal with challenging environmental conditions, giving us tools, such as dowsing, to help us live in the world harmoniously, healthily, and happily. All we have to do is use them.

Lori had more to share with her friends, but wanted to

wait for the effects of this process to sink in. She was aware that every step was taking each of them closer to the love they desired. But she didn't feel in a hurry. She was enjoying this journey.

One of the attributes of love, like art, is to

bring harmony and order out of chaos, to

introduce meaning and affect where before

there was none, to give rhythmic variations,

highs, and lows to a landscape that was

previously flat.

—MOLLY HASKELL

CHAPTER ELEVEN

Appreciation and Blessings: Creating Harmony

One of the challenges of relationships, which prevents many people from pursuing them, is poor communication and the stress that builds when unnamed tensions arise.

Just as energy gets stuck in the physical environment, it can get stuck in relationships, too. From a Vastu perspective, when two people argue a lot and generally disagree, their energies get caught in a pattern that exists in both people and lodges within the physical structure of the space they share. Over time, the home or workplace where the discord happens develops an aura of uneasiness that anyone who enters can feel. When underlying tension has never been cleared, it's easy to become depressed or angry in such an environment.

Here is a lovely practice and a wonderful clearing ceremony that releases this stuck energy. It will help you feel uplifted and peaceful in your relationships at home and at work. When the time comes, you can share it with Mr. Right.

Action Step 9a
The Art of Appreciation

In every relationship the stress from everyday living intrudes. It might become difficult for one or both people to be present emotionally, heart open. In times such as these, isn't your true desire to let go of disappointment, sadness, and other emotions that make you feel separate from those you love? Don't you wish there was a surefire way to reconnect?

The following process reunites couples, or others in close relationship such as family members or friends, who experience disconnection. You can use this process when there is some unresolved hurt, frustration, or unfulfilled expectation that prevents you from being close to another. It will help you to keep the lines of communication and your hearts open, and assist you to see each other without past hurts and disappointments clouding the reality of your love for each other.

Each person will have an opportunity to speak, one at a time. The person who is not speaking listens attentively, without interrupting the other person. This is a time to be receptive, not defensive, when listening. For some, this openness will take discipline.

MICHAEL'S VASTU TIP: Practice keeping your full attention on your partner. When you feel your mind engaging, or you desire to interrupt because something doesn't feel right, instead of doing this, take a deep breath in and out. This will help you relax and move the energy that is getting stuck in either your heart or your mind.

THE PROCESS

❋ Sit facing your partner.

❋ The first person will speak of what she **appreciates** about the second person, as the second person listens. When the first person has said everything she wishes to say, you switch roles: the second person says everything he appreciates about the first.

✾ The next topic is about what you **resent** about the other person—what that person has, in your opinion, done that you feel badly about. The second person again listens. Then you switch roles.

✾ The third topic is about what you **regret** has happened in the relationship. Again, as the first person speaks, the second listens. Then you switch.

✾ The fourth topic focuses on what you **wish** could be so. For example, once you have cleared what you regret, you might wish to spend more time together or treat each other more lovingly. Remember to say everything that comes to mind. Again, switch roles.

✾ The fifth and final topic comes full circle, back once again to say what you **appreciate** about this person sitting in front of you. You will find at this point that most of the frustrations and stress with which you began this exercise have dissipated, and your appreciation of the person opposite you will have a very different quality. You might notice it being more heartfelt. Switch roles again.

THE CHOICE IS YOURS

What is most important to remember is that in every moment, you have the choice of whether to choose love. When you put love first, dropping all thoughts of control, thoughts of having the upper hand, and the desire to be right, you create an opportunity for healing and growth. This choice says you want to be fearless in your vulnerability and willingly embrace not only the other, but also yourself. This vulnerability is the greatest kind of power, as it reveals your authentic self, without bravado, defense, or righteousness. True power lies in surrendering your personal agendas of the mind for the betterment of your personal growth; it is the ability to remain open and available to the magic that comes from putting love above all else.

Action Step 9b
The Blessing Ceremony

This ceremony is of great benefit and can transform your home into a haven where relationships grow and thrive. It can be used after you have cleared geopathic stress and/or when you want an extra energetic boost of support in attracting Mr. Right. You also can use it when any relationship feels blocked or stagnated. This procedure also honors the five elements of earth, air, water, fire, and space, uplifting the energy in the environment and bringing balance and harmony into your life.

THE PREPARATION

The following items are representative of the five elements. They will be placed on a clean, round, small tray that can easily be carried in one hand as you make your way throughout your home.

* Place the tray in front of you as you face **east**. The elements are placed in a specific pattern on the tray.

* In the lower left-hand side—the northwest sector of your tray—place incense in a small incense holder. You can use the scent of ylang-ylang, which calms the mind and opens the heart, or sandalwood, whose sweet fragrance uplifts the spirit and brings peace. Incense is symbolic of the air element, which supports attraction, change, and movement.

* In the upper left-hand side—the northeast area of your tray—place a container, such as a small

bowl or teacup, of purified water. The water element symbolizes growth and intimacy in relationships.

❀ Use a candle in the color red to rekindle or ignite passion, or pink to open the heart to receive love. Place the candle in the upper right-hand side of the tray. This area symbolizes the southeast and the fire element. It represents the passion needed for stimulating or renewing relationships, and the illumination of the self as partner within the relationship.

❀ Place a small bowl of uncooked rice on the tray in the lower right-hand side to symbolize the earth element. This element represents the support needed to establish and maintain a successful relationship. As part of the ceremony, you will be sprinkling a few grains of rice in each room to ground the stabilizing energy needed for a relationship to grow.

❀ In the center of the tray, place a small bell. A bell represents the space element and, when rung, focuses your attention by bringing your awareness to the present moment. You will ring the bell in each room and as you move throughout your home during this ceremony. The sound invites the divine energy of harmony, or relationship success, into each room.

❀ Place a small flower, such as a daisy or a carnation, on any side of the tray. The flower should not be too delicate, as you will be dipping it into the cup of water to sprinkle a few drops of water in each room as a symbolic gesture of purification.

❀ Review the mantras in chapter 7. Decide which one resonates with you most easily and then chant that mantra throughout the following ceremony. (You may change to another mantra the next time you perform the ceremony.)

THE CEREMONY

You will be walking through your home beginning in the northwest and continuing in a clockwise motion through each room, ending in the west. As you enter individual rooms, you'll walk clockwise through them, beginning at the door and then proceeding out of the room.

As you perform this ceremony, envision each room filled with love, joy, and laughter. As you enter each room, chant the mantra you have chosen three times as you take your flower, dip it into the cup of water, and sprinkle the water a few times into the air. Ring the bell a few times, allowing the sound to linger and dissipate before you ring it again. Before leaving the room, take a few grains of rice and drop them to the floor by the entrance of the door. See the grains of rice as seeds you are planting for the future you wish to create. Using this ceremony, you have created sacred space and blessed it with your dreams and longings for a future filled with the love, grace, and ease you desire.

Finally, please contemplate—really think about—these principles:

Appreciate differences. When you accept another with all that person's unique vulnerabilities and differences, you dwell in the heart rather than in your mind. The heart is a much gentler, loving place for you to reside.

Embrace your future with your arms open wide. Keep your heart open, your mind alert, and say "yes" to each and every moment.

Offer every doubt to the divine. So often our biggest challenge comes from the doubting mind that questions and analyzes what is yet to come. Whenever your mind doubts your future or your ability to be happy, stop the inner chatter and offer those self-defeating thoughts and fears to the divine. The mastery is to live in the present moment, which is the most wonderful present the divine has given you.

Sasha, Lori, and Faith are getting together to discuss the processes for revitalizing relationships and purifying the environment. Let's see what they discover from sharing their experiences about the morning rituals, too.

Opening the Heart and the Home: Making Room for Love

One late, rainy afternoon after work, Lori and Charlene saw each other in the parking garage of the hospital where they worked. They decided to have tea and discuss the changes that had happened since Lori introduced Charlene to Vastu.

CHARLENE

Carving out time for her social life was a major focus for Charlene. And learning to put some fun back into her life had begun to yield some interesting results. She felt better, more relaxed, and more present with what was before her to do. Lately she had begun to catch herself whenever she found herself worrying, and instead focused on her new mantra: Stop worrying and enjoy life. It seemed to be working.

As they had discussed on the group shopping trip, Charlene had done several of the techniques, and she had begun to feel real change. She had identified major stressors in her life and had set about to relieve herself of some of that stress.

"I hired a new assistant," she told Lori. "She's a whiz and has taken over some of the busywork. So, on that front, I'm feeling more relaxed. The boys are doing well in school, and things are going a lot more smoothly at home in general. I have you to thank for that! The biggest change has been in my attitude.

"Ever since I put my Relationship Altar together, I've been feeling so much happier. I think it's also taking the time every day to do some yoga and those mantras you taught me. Every time I add some of the other practices and suggestions, I feel a wave of appreciation for my life and this feeling of love just wells up inside. At first it was startling. It caught me off guard. Do you know what I mean?" She looked at Lori for validation.

Lori knew just how Charlene felt. You also might feel this when you open yourself with these tools and techniques: it's gratitude. This overflowing sense of thankfulness is our natural state; its essence is self-love, not in a selfish way but in a sacred way. The grace and gratitude occur when you honor what is inside you and your connection to the divine.

Charlene went on to tell Lori that she still felt her relationship with her husband was stuck. Lori shared with her the Art of Appreciation and the wonderful dialogue that Charlene and Daniel could have with each other. "My feeling," Lori explained, "is that men and women definitely have differences in communication. This process puts us on an equal playing field and gives both a way to speak from the heart and clear the air.

"Some people have told me they do it in twenty minutes or a half hour, and others take longer. You take as long as you need," Lori continued. "All I can say is, it works not only for your intimate relationship, but you can do it with the boys, too, when things start going haywire with them. I do it with Emma and Ava whenever I feel frustrated or resentful, when I feel those not-so-pleasant emotions building up. This process does clear the air and open your heart. Give it a try and let me know if you notice anything."

She then told Charlene about the Blessing Ceremony, which can be used all by itself or after you clear the emotional air with the Art of Appreciation.

After going through what was needed for the Blessing Ceremony and as they said their good-byes, Charlene thanked Lori for being a good friend. "I'm telling everyone I know about what you've given me, girlfriend. I hope you're all right with me spreading the word."

Lori smiled. "Of course! In fact, when we do the next Full Moon Ceremony, please bring anyone you want to. We really want to share this with the community."

"That's so good." Charlene felt a wave of possibility run through her. "It's much needed."

Two days later, Charlene told Lori that she and Daniel had done both processes. Voicing their frustrations and acknowledgments had been cathartic, Charlene said. Daniel had even agreed to come to the next Full Moon Ceremony with her, seeing the benefit in everything Lori had shared with Charlene so far.

"I'm so glad that this is helping you," exclaimed Lori. "Adding this new dimension to your relationship is not only going to affect your marriage, but also it will have a ripple effect in other areas of your lives."

FAITH, SASHA, AND LORI CHECK IN

When Lori shared all the details of the processes with Faith and Sasha, they were open to using them.

LORI

The women shared with each other about the practices they had integrated into their lives each morning, and then Faith brought the conversation back to focus on Lori.

Having Ben back in her life felt easy and right, Lori told her friends. Ava and Emma had included him right from the start, just like he was family. Lori had forgotten what it was like being with a man who cared.

"Ben never really stopped loving me," she said. "He was always the most supportive person in my life, besides my parents. He encouraged me in all my dreams and had an open and fair way of treating not only me, but everyone. He's that kind of person.

"I've shared with him all the things you two and I have been doing together. He's asked a lot of great questions and finds the science of Vastu fascinating. He also wanted to come to the Full Moon Ceremony."

Both Sasha and Faith were happy that Lori found someone so well suited for her. This is what came to Lori for all she had done for herself and others—love—in the form of a beautiful man who was just right for her.

FAITH

Faith was having a delightful relationship with herself and had learned to trust her intuition before jumping into a relationship with a man too quickly, no matter how tempted she felt in the moment. She had been on a date with Avery—a *real* date, she mused. And they had a fabulous time. He treated her like she sincerely mattered, and she liked how that felt.

Lori knew the kind of journey Faith had been on and how she used to treat herself. "I applaud you for your growth, Faith. I've known you for a long time, but this time we're in right now is where I've seen your wings unfold and watched you fly. It's lovely," Lori said as the emotion caught in her throat. "Really and truly, lovely."

Faith had transformed herself. The three of them had.

SASHA

Sasha and Elliott had talked about taking a vacation together, maybe visiting his family in Chicago. She was nervous about it but wanted to go.

"I think when it comes to love," Faith told her, "the timing is always perfect. I really do. Each relationship has its own timing and rhythm. You've got to let it unfold and be willing to take a few risks. Perfection is one thing that rarely exists side by side with emotional happiness on planet Earth."

With the next Full Moon Ceremony coming up, the friends were looking forward to welcoming a whole new group of people into their little circle. Faith and Mary had invited Alice and some other people from the church's singles group, and Sasha had invited people from her staff at work. Most of them had wanted to include a friend or two as well. With Lori's yoga class and a few other friends from work, they were looking at close to sixty joining them for the event. It would be a mixture of young and old, married and single, men and women, all coming together to open their hearts and expand their lives in celebration and possibility.

Love is everything it's cracked up to be.

That's why people are so cynical about it. It

really is worth fighting for, being brave for,

risking everything for. And the trouble is, if

you don't risk anything, you risk even more.

—ERICA JONG

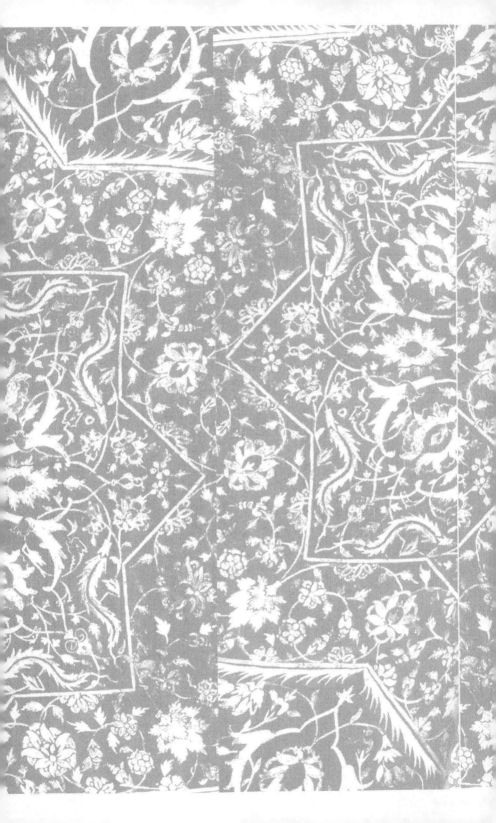

CHAPTER TWELVE

Creating Love Through Power and Purpose

When you live in harmony with the natural forces and elements, you feel the abundant love and support that exist everywhere. As Vastu demonstrates over and over again, the universe is benevolent and continually offers us the power to be happy and fulfilled.

We have covered many subjects in this book, and hope that we have inspired you to practice if not all, at least some of the techniques of Vastu. Clearing clutter is essential. We also hope that you will eliminate geopathic stress in your home and office. While dowsing may be considered a secondary technique, it is so effective that we wouldn't think of moving into a new home or office without checking for this kind of stress.

Likewise, the Process of Attraction, which is a decluttering of your inner world, forms a space within you that can be filled with the great energy of divine love that your Vastu work allows to flow unimpeded through your life.

Vastu is not magic, but its influence and effects can be magical if you apply them. Energy exists and the elements exist; these facts cannot be denied. How you connect with them determines your future.

Whether you begin to use these practices and see results immediately or begin and seem to notice nothing different, have faith! Trust that you are connected to the benevolent force that wants you to realize your most precious desires. You may struggle with finding time for the action steps, but just by giving it your best you will find shifts happening and eventually fulfillment. We are certain of this. Keep your mind and heart open, have faith that you are connected to the divine, and you will notice the signs that Mr. Right is on his way into your life.

On the evening of the next full moon, Faith, Lori, Sasha, Mary, Charlene, and Corrine greeted a host of people at the yoga studio for their celebration. Faith, Mary, and

Sasha had set up a three-tiered altar on an Indian rug. They used crates and storage containers to build the altar and then covered it with pink sheets. They placed the elements of earth, air, water, and fire on the lower tiers. On the very top tier, which was smaller than the other two, they placed a silver tray, symbolic of the space element, for everyone to place the three words that synthesized their desires for the coming month.

The altar came together quickly, and the women stood back from time to time to admire it. There was plenty of room on the lower two tiers for the offerings that people would bring to be energized that evening. Faith brought the collage of the men she had framed for the last Full Moon Ceremony.

She had invited Avery and Chris to the event. She was very aware of the fact that by focusing on feeling full within herself she had attracted two kindhearted, happy men who made her laugh and had wonderful minds and spirits.

Faith also had a knack for decorating and brought a collection of things to enhance the beauty of the altar. Ben came, and so did Sasha's new love. There were other men there, some with women, and some came single—a very mixed group in age and background.

Lori was waiting for the moment to step up as the

spokesperson and for the event to begin when she noticed, standing against a wall in the back of the room, the collage of men Faith had made for the first altar ceremony. She retrieved it, held it up, and caught Faith's eye. They both laughed as Faith walked over to her. "Oh, I guess I forgot to place it on the altar." She sighed, looking at the bright, smiling faces framed together. "I can't believe how different today feels than the day I made this," Faith added, remembering the day so clearly. "It wasn't that long ago—at least in time it doesn't seem that long ago—but it's like aeons have passed when I think about everything that's gone on since then."

Sasha approached and smiled, taking the collage from Lori. "Lovely-looking men," Sasha said, shaking her head in amazement. "Well, all I can say is that it works. At least it worked for me and for both of you."

"And it will work for others, too. All we have to do is lead by example. How else does anyone really learn?" Lori looked at her two friends, feeling the strength and love each of them had. "If it doesn't come from our own experience, it's empty talk. I think people have had enough of that. We all want the same things—to love and be loved, to know we're not alone, and that there is something, some presence that listens and cares and is there for us always. Haven't we proven to ourselves and each other that all those things do exist and are true?" She looked from Sasha to Faith, seeing the appreciation in her friends' eyes. "Mark my words," Lori said as she caught Ben's eye from across the room, "this is just the beginning of something wonderful."

As Lori stepped up before the group, she felt a surge of excitement. "I'd like to welcome everyone," she said with a smile, realizing how right it felt to be surrounded by old friends and new, all there to share their heart's desires. "We're so happy to see you here, and I personally hope that you will enjoy the benefits that I have found and that my friends Faith and Sasha, Mary, Charlene, and Corrine also have experienced from using Vastu. I have no idea what's going to happen as a result of this gathering, but I do know that it will be great. And I sincerely hope you will join us again at the next full moon to do this again."

Lori then explained the power of altars and the importance of setting intention. She described the process of offering the three words and of energizing the altar. Because the group was so large, they would do each step together. "I think that it would be appropriate to set the intentions for this ceremony to be peace, love, and fulfillment to all for the coming month," she added.

As she looked out at the group, she saw a little fear, perhaps, but mostly hope, kindness, happiness, and anticipation in the beautiful faces that looked back at her. She smiled at Ben and the others and offered a quick, silent prayer in her heart of blessings, love, and thanks for all that had been and for the adventures yet to come.

The purpose of life, after all, is to live it,

to taste experience to the utmost,

to reach out eagerly and without fear

for newer, and richer experience.

—ELEANOR ROOSEVELT

Acknowledgments

What a blessing it has been to write this book! From its inception, it made us smile and feel great gratitude for its message of hope as it flew onto the pages. What began as a dream became a reality, and infused with our prayers, we hope it will find its way into your life and heart.

It is clear that the time for its message is now.

Everyone who helped with this book did so with the most generous and heartfelt loving spirit. We can't thank you enough for all your enthusiastic encouragement and support. From our friends and families to our colleagues, teachers, clients, and students—you've cheered us on, believing in our vision that maybe by loving self first, finding trust and hope first, surrendering fear and disappointment now, women would try a new way, a new direction to fulfill their heart's desires.

Thank you Judith Curr and Malaika Adero for believing in our vision and making our experience at Simon & Schuster and Atria Books a dream-filled adventure. Malaika, you are a masterful editorial magician and a delight to know and work with. Your patience and enthusiasm are blessings in our lives. And to everyone at Simon & Schuster and Atria Books who has enthusiastically embraced the vision of our work and has given it their loving attention and continued support, we bow down to you. What you bring to the table is deeply felt by us. We are very grateful and thank you with all our heart.

We also are very grateful for the steadfast, creative support of our editor and friend Terry Hiller, who came into our lives through the spiritual network that has been a part of all our books. Thank you for your dedication and your curiosity. How wonderful for all of us that the power of this book was validated as it brought positive changes into your life in the process of its creation. A heartfelt thank you goes to Judy Mikalonis for her superb editorial and marketing expertise. Also, to our youngest daughter, Amy, for her astute eye and fabulous way with words, thank you for your editing assistance. To Valerie Sensabaugh, the queen of final edits, your support has been invaluable. Finally, to our dear friend, teacher of teachers, and artist supreme, the one constant in all our books: Scott Hague. Your creative genius and sweet spirit can be felt in every drawing within these pages. You are always there for us, willing to jump in and help without hesitation. A million blessings, divine one!

We'd like to acknowledge our dear friends Camille and Peter Stranger, Brenda Michaels and Rob Spears, DiVanna VaDree, Dean Thompson and David Rothmiller, Molly Linton, Margaret Lanz, Lori Ehrig, Molly Murrah, Vicki Garland, June Martin, Deja Hanson, Rekha and Ravi Baldwada, Connie and Tim Hipsher, John and Arrieanna Thompson, Liza Davis, Ann Craig, and so many more . . . thank you for your encouragement, contributions, and love.

Sunny Sumter deserves a special mention here because it was her sweet insistence that opened literary doors with such grace and ease. You had a feeling, and the time was right.

To our teachers, especially Sri Sri Ravi Shankar, Maharishi Mahesh Yogi, Vaidya Mishra, Vaidya Priyanka, and Mary Jo Cravatta, thank you for your encouragement and support of our work around the world.

Lastly, we thank our family for their continued support and encouragement in all our work.

We are, without a doubt, very blessed and filled with gratitude for all the love and grace that flow in our lives.

Resources

CHAPTER 2

Here are only a few of the many online dating services available on the World Wide Web:

http://www.match.com

http://www.greatexpectations.com

http://www.eharmony.com

CHAPTER 5

Information on altars:

http://www.vastucreations.com

CHAPTER 6

Spiritual practices:

    http://us.artofliving.org

    http://www.tm.org

Information on altars:

    http://www.vastucreations.com

Additional yantras for your Relationship Altar:

    http://www.vastucreations.com

CHAPTER 7

Web site for downloadable yantras, mantras, and guided meditation:

    http://www.makingroomformrright.com

Web site to purchase statues and yantras:

    http://www.vastucreations.com

CHAPTER 8

Web sites about color:

    http://www.behr.com/behrx/inspiration/emotional_8.jsp

    http://www.sensationalcolor.com/index.php

Web sites for gems and stones:

> *http://www.rockras.com/gemstone-properties/*
>
> *http://www.wondrousgems.com (Click on Gemstone Properties FAQ)*
>
> *http://oliadesigns.com/stones.php*
>
> *http://www.peacefulmind.com*
>
> *http://www.mineralminers.com*

Web sites and book for essential oils:

> *http://www.care2.com/greenliving/best-essential-oils-for-love.html*
>
> *http://storeswalk-in-beauty.net*
>
> *Reference Guide for Essential Oils*, 9th ed., compiled by Connie and Alan Higley. Spanish Fork, Utah: Abundant Health, 1998–2005.
>
> *http://Walk-in-Beauty.net*

CHAPTER 9

Tongue scraping:

> *http://www.yatan-ayur.com.au/tongue_scrapers.htm*

http://en.wikipedia.org/wiki/Ama (Click on Ama, Ayurveda)

http://www.wellbeing.com.au/natural_health_ articles?cid=7733&pid=2149492

Abhyanga:

http://www.shaktiveda.com/index.html

http://www.vaidyamishra.com

http://www.sattvaspa.com/ancient_ayurvedic_ treatments.html

http://www.youthingstrategies.com

Oil pulling:

http://en.wikipedia.org/wiki/Oil_pulling

http://www.earthclinic.com/Remedies/oil_pulling. html

http://www.oilpulling.com

Yoga:

http://www.yogawiz.com

http://www.healthandyoga.com/html/yoga/Benefits. html

Sudarshan kriya:

http://us.artofliving.org

Meditation:

http://www.tm.org

http://us.artofliving.org

CHAPTER 10

http://en.wikipedia.org/wiki/Geopathic_Stress

http://www.healingcancernaturally.com/geopathic-stress-and-cancer.html

Quotes throughout the book:

http://www.romantic-lyrics.com/lovequotes14.shtml

http://www.wisdomquotes.com/cat_love.html